P9-EMB-693

Applied
Strategies
for Curriculum
Evaluation

CARNEGIE LIBRARY
LIVINGSTONE COLLEGE
SALISBURY, N. C. 28144

Ronald S. Brandt, Editor

Association for Supervision and Curriculum Development
225 North Washington Street, Alexandria, Virginia 22314

121293

Editing:
Ronald S. Brandt, ASCD Executive Editor
Nancy Carter Modrak, Managing Editor, Booklets

Cover design: Great Incorporated

Copyright © 1981 by the Association for Supervision and Curriculum Development. All rights reserved. No part of this publication may be reproduced or transmitted in any form or by any means, electronic or mechanical, including photocopy, recording, or any information storage and retrieval system, without permission in writing from the publisher.

The materials printed herein are the expressions of the writers and not necessarily a statement of policy of the Association.

Stock number: 611-81240
Library of Congress Catalog Card Number: 81-68494
ISBN: 0-87120-108-9

Contents

Foreword / iv
Lucille G. Jordan

Introduction / vi
Ronald S. Brandt

1. **The Evaluator's Curse / 1**
   W. James Popham

2. **Five Phases of Purposeful Inquiry / 9**
   Deborah G. Bonnet

3. **Evaluating Responsively / 25**
   Robert E. Stake and James A. Pearsol

4. **The Radnor Evaluation Derby / 34**
   Michael Scriven

5. **Using Professional Judgment / 41**
   Elliot W. Eisner

6. **CIPP in Local Evaluation / 48**
   William J. Webster

7. **Journal Entries of an Eclectic Evaluator / 58**
   Blaine R. Worthen

Groping for the Elephant / 91
Henry M. Brickell

Appendix A / 104
A Short History of the Radnor Middle School Humanities Curriculum
William P. Byrne and Mark A. Springer

Appendix B / 108
Report of the Humanities Curriculum Review Committee

Foreword

As professional educators, we are schooled in the importance of building into every program plan an evaluation component. Even when an evaluation has not been solicited, most of us feel an urgency to pass judgment on programs, activities, products, and participants. Yet too often we do little more than deal with surface factors when we fail to commit ourselves to developing evaluation plans that can yield the most appropriate data for the decisions that must be made.

Developing just such a plan was the challenging assignment of the contributors to this booklet. With a few documents giving background information and without actually observing the curriculum in process, the authors describe how they would go about evaluating a middle school humanities program. They tell us how they would identify information needs and set priorities, how they would obtain information from a variety of sources, and what they would do with the data they collect in terms of formulating recommendations and suggestions for the school board. Each author is experienced in evaluation in the affective domain and each emphasizes his or her value position.

The variety of evaluation approaches they present should prove especially helpful in supplying alternatives for program planners. The questions the authors raise are on target and prompt critical thinking. For instance:

- Exactly how will the findings of this evaluation plan be raised?
- What decisions are to be made considering these data and who will make those decisions?
- What benefits does this program produce at what cost?
- What is the relationship between what was planned and what is being implemented?
- Do the learning experiences of this program displace others of higher value or priority?

One process response to these questions is the use of the adversarial evaluation approach; that is, using two evaluators who take opposing views, or contrasting the opinions of supporters and detractors of the program and selecting appropriate data to substantiate each opinion.

Realistically, we know that program impact is always indicated in broader terms than the data show. However, one of the spin-off values of a good evaluation plan is the necessity to keep goals in constant visibility. We have all observed educationally significant program outcomes that would never show statistical significance because their side effects cannot be constrained in the limits of prescribed instructional objectives.

Some of the other "blue chip" stocks the writers emphasize are the importance of establishing trust between all groups involved in an evaluation; finalizing agreements between evaluator and client about deadlines, budgets, and specific steps to be taken; and holding a client review to identify inaccuracies and to challenge inferences and recommendations before the final evaluation report is presented.

Evaluation is the process of making meaning out of experience and converting experience into meaningful behavior, which results in better learning programs. The appropriate evaluation plan provides the right information to the right persons in the right way for them to make the right decisions.

LUCILLE G. JORDAN
President, 1981-82
Association for Supervision
and Curriculum Development

Introduction

"How have you evaluated this program?" asked the president of the board of education. She seemed determined to maintain an air of objectivity, but the atmosphere was growing tense in the school library where the board was meeting.

The main business of the evening was a report on the middle school's humanities program. Prepared by a committee of 11 educators and six parents, the report was the product of more than 30 committee meetings plus discussions with students, staff, and citizens, and correspondence with other schools. It explained philosophy, listed goals and objectives, described the curriculum in detail,[1] made specific recommendations, and included a rationale for each recommendation. It even listed a number of alternatives that had been considered, but which were rejected as undesirable.

All students in the sixth, seventh, and eighth grades were required to take the humanities course, which was taught two days a week by four teachers, including an artist and a musician, all members of a separate humanities department. The arts—everything from literature, drama, film, music, and dance, to architecture and the visual arts—were used to develop the students' "understanding of all that it means to be human." Looking at a Van Gogh painting of a Flemish mining family at dinner, for instance, students might be asked, "Would you like to be invited to dinner here?" as well as, "What tones and colors did the painter use?" They might listen to Humperdink's opera, *Hansel and Gretel,* or "She's Leaving Home," by the Beatles. Examples were drawn from African and Oriental cultures as well as from European and American.

---

[1] See Appendix B, beginning at page 108.

The program should be continued, the report said, with some modifications, including a new organizational framework based on the concepts and skills being taught, and increased emphasis on writing and other language skills.

Several board members and parents were not satisfied. A woman who was a member of the study committee, but who had not attended most meetings, read a statement expressing concern about the general direction of American education and objected to "values clarification" and "secular humanism" in the program.[2]

Others said a humanities course would be more appropriate for older students, who would have the background to appreciate it, but that students in the middle school needed more basic knowledge first. One board member asked what impact the program was having on students and how it could be measured.

Pointing out that the program had been in limbo for more than a year, the principal, assistant superintendent for curriculum, and the superintendent gave strong personal endorsement and asked for an immediate decision. Several parents added their support. But when the meeting ended at 11:00 p.m., the board had postponed acceptance of the committee's report until they could talk privately with the principal about how the program could be scheduled and staffed in light of declining enrollments.

Ten days later, a majority of the board members voted to permit continuation of the humanities course. Still, evaluation remained an issue. In reply to the question about measurement, the principal had said it couldn't be done statistically; the course did not teach children *what* to think and feel, it taught them *to* think and feel.

The humanities curriculum at Radnor Middle School is unusual, but the situation I have described is not. In school districts throughout the United States, parents and citizens are questioning the worth of school programs. Unusual courses or activities are especially suspect; taxpayers and parents naturally wonder why one school district should have them if others do not. But conventional courses are also questioned, especially if they seem ineffective.

Patrons aren't the only ones interested in evaluation, of course. Educators also want to know more about the value of the programs they offer. Unfortunately, shoddy evaluation may be worse than none at all, and quality evaluation is expensive and difficult.

Knowing that few school districts can afford to hire noted authorities

---

[2] The teachers insisted they did not use techniques such as those advocated by Simon, Howe, and Kirschenbaum in *Values Clarification: A Handbook of Practical Strategies for Teachers and Students* (New York: Hart, 1972).

to evaluate their programs, we invited six experts to describe what they might do if they were asked to evaluate the Radnor humanities curriculum. Their comments are enlightening. The issues they would address, the questions they would ask, the data they would seek, and the way they would gather it are different in some respects but similar in others. Their comments offer an array of interesting possibilities for consideration by local evaluators.

You may be surprised to find so much humor in a book about such a serious subject. Worthen and Popham, particularly, though as much in earnest as the other authors, use a delightfully playful style. And the final chapter, in which Henry ("Mitch") Brickell wittily analyzes the advice of his fellow evaluators, makes a rich dessert.

All of this may or may not be helpful to Radnor, but it should be immensely useful to the rest of us.

RONALD S. BRANDT
Executive Editor
Association for Supervision
and Curriculum Development

1.
The Evaluator's Curse

by W. James Popham

With his emphasis on precisely-worded behavioral objectives and well-crafted criterion-referenced tests, James Popham represents the measurement tradition in educational evaluation. As in this chapter, he often flavors his writing with a dash of humor. Popham is Professor of Education, University of California, Los Angeles.

Evaluating a humanities program holds challenges akin to those involved in evaluating a formal religion. Architects of both enterprises really don't believe their efforts can possibly be evaluated here on earth. Whereas the religionist contends that genuine payoffs to the devout occur only in an afterlife, proponents of the humanities often garb their programs in such effusive rhetoric that evaluators dare approach their appraisal task only with well warranted trembling.

Consider, for example, the modest aspirations of the humanities program at Radnor Middle School. As a consequence of two classes per week, it is expected that students will increase their aesthetic sensibilities, critical thinking skills, appreciation of human achievement in the arts, appreciation of their own and others' cultural heritages, understanding of the interrelatedness among disparate disciplines—not to mention their communication skills. That's a pretty big bundle. In contrast, the cleric's task of spiriting folks through the Pearly Gates seems fairly modest.

It is because humanities educators have such unbridled enthusiasm and lofty aspirations for their programs that they view the efforts of evaluators with automatic suspicion. "How," they ask, "can anyone possibly assess the power and richness of our programs? After all, we are helping children search for answers to basic questions about life."

It is this incredulity which, for me, makes the evaluation of a humanities program so challenging. It's an opportunity to convert a few non-believers (in evaluation). Beyond that, there's the challenge of coming up with legitimate ways of capturing the difficult-to-gauge outcomes of a humanities program. After all, it's loads easier to measure a pupil's ability to perform arithmetic computations than it is to tap the "ability to respond both affectively and cognitively to a variety of aesthetic experiences."

On reflection, perhaps we should create an evaluator's version of the ancient Chinese curse, "May you live in interesting times." The modern day paraphrase, designed to damn today's educational evaluators, might run as follows: *"May your evaluation projects be challenging."*

Model Molding

When the other chapter contributors and I were asked to set forth our approaches to evaluating the Radnor humanities program, we were each urged to use our own evaluation "model." That request troubled me somewhat, since I have never really set forth a published step-by-step version of my personal procedural preferences for carrying out an educational evaluation.

A good many writers, of course, have already produced some first-rate evaluation models. Dan Stufflebeam and Egon Guba gave us their well known CIPP Model. Bob Stake's early writings provided us with the Countenance Model. And Michael Scriven has given us his Olympian Model (since he spends a fair amount of mountain-top time in consort with Zeus and other deities). Given these already established and highly useful models, I never really felt compelled to churn out my own.

Besides, what would I call it? There's precious little allure in referring to something as Popham's Model. I suppose I could abbreviate it, but the initials P.M. have already been staked out by those who like to tell time. Perhaps I could try Popham's Procedure, but that abbreviation is even worse. Let's face it, I'm too late. There are enough evaluation models around already. Fate has placed the task of building evaluation models in better hands than mine. Hence, please don't think of what follows as an attempt to describe a formal evaluation model.

As I thought about the Radnor humanities program and the approach I would use in evaluating it, I realized there are two basic operations I always engage in when conducting an educational evaluation. First, I try to get the decisions at issue clearly out on the table so all can see. Second, having clarified the decision options under review, I assemble as much meaningful data as possible that might reasonably bear on those decisions. Somebody has to make a decision, and that decision will be made judgmentally. I want to enhance that judgment by filling the decision makers' skulls with pertinent sorts of data.

Clarifying the decision at issue is more difficult than most people realize. Frequently, there are multiple decision makers who are operating in the context of differing decision frameworks. Clarification of the decision often forces these individuals to resolve their previously unrecognized disagreements.

There's another dividend to be gained by pushing for decision clarity: by requiring the decision to be isolated, we can avoid "evaluation as ritual" and "evaluation for interest."

Some evaluations are carried out almost ritualistically in the belief that since evaluation is an intrinsically praiseworthy endeavor, it ought to be done. Those who carry out "evaluation as ritual" really don't intend to do anything very meaningful with the results. Because they reason that truly worthwhile programs are always accompanied these days by evaluations, they're satisfied with having done an evaluation.

Other educators carry out evaluation to discern if anything interesting happened during or after a program. They are content to conclude that one or more elements of the program were "interesting" or "thought-provoking." These folks, like the proponents of ritualistic evaluation, don't really intend to take action based on the results of the evaluation. Nonetheless, like the ritualistic evaluators, they can be dissuaded from impactless evaluations by having the decisions at issue clearly staked out and well publicized before the evaluation.

Turning to the assembly of pertinent information, there's a good deal of artistry involved. Skillful evaluators have to consider the nature of the decision, then quest for a range of data that, based on their training and experience, appear to be germane. For example, if the decisions were focused on program improvement (calling for what Scriven terms *formative* evaluation), then I'd gather plenty of information about the way the program was being implemented. It's tough to shape up a treatment if you don't know what the treatment actually is. If, on the other hand, the decision were focused on continuing versus terminating a program (calling for Scriven's *summative* evaluation), I'd give more attention to evidence regarding the program's effects.

In the process of clarifying decision options and garnering relevant information, there are all sorts of wrinkles we've learned about over the last decade or so. I'll try to illustrate the use of some of these in relation to Radnor Middle School's humanities endeavors.

The Decision at Issue

Having been told that chapter contributors could telephone the Radnor Middle School principal, Anne Janson, for additional information, I took advantage of the early morning telephone rates and reached her prior to sunrise in Los Angeles. Her answers to my questions were forthright and illuminating. I hope that in the analysis to follow I can do credit to her insights.

Not surprisingly, my first question to Mrs. Janson was, "Is the Radnor board of education the decision-making group in your situation and, if so, what is the nature of the decision or decisions at issue?" She thought for a moment, then indicated that the board members were clearly the decision makers, and that the decision they seemed to be contemplating was whether or not to continue the humanities program at Radnor. She pointed out that some board members had expressed concern about whether it is appropriate for children this young to study humanities. More fundamental, she felt, was the belief by some board members that the time devoted by the middle school's students to humanities could be better spent on the acquisition of more basic skills, such as reading and mathematics, or in treating more fundamental knowledge such as social studies or science.

Based on Mrs. Janson's observations, I was convinced the situation called for a summative, rather than formative, evaluation. I should add that if I actually were to carry out this evaluation in Radnor, I would spend substantial time querying the board members personally, for I would be anxious to make certain that the go/no go decision was the only one they had in mind regarding the humanities program.

Data Delving

Having isolated the nature of the decision context, the next task in my evaluation would be to decide what sorts of information the decision makers might need in order to come up with an absolutely Solomon-like judgment regarding whether to save or scrap the program. This is the point at which evaluators with a low I.Q. (Ingenuity Quotient) had best abandon the challenges of appraising humanities programs and return instead to programs fostering students' spelling skills.

First I'd talk to all members of the board to identify what sorts of criteria, if any, they might have in mind when they contemplate a save/scrap decision regarding the program. In this situation I have relied on Mrs. Janson's insights regarding what she thought might be of significance to board members. She believed they would be persuaded of the humanities program's worth if evidence could be marshalled showing the program was enhancing youngsters' basic skills, such as reading or writing. She also thought board members would be attentive to evidence regarding some of the affective objectives of the program, if it were possible to secure valid indications of student affect regarding the humanities.

I can certainly see why the school board might want a pile of evidence in reaching their decision, particularly since they'd been barraged with a pile of rhetoric in the 1979 report of the Humanities Curriculum Review Committee. That committee, whose membership we might surmise was tilted toward the virtues of the humanities program, had set forth a series of hurrahs for humanities without a scrap of evidence. I am not suggesting that it was the mission of the committee to gather data; undoubtedly it wasn't. But if I were a Radnor board member, I'd be a bit wary of those offering such one-sided and extravagant claims. I'd want less enthusiasm and more hard evidence that the humanities program was worth its salt.

Before turning to the thorny problem of whether there's a legitimate data-gathering design, which would permit us to draw valid inferences from the administration of particular measuring instruments, let's see if we can come up with the necessary instruments themselves.

There would seem to be two major classes of outcome evidence in which we should be interested here: cognitive and affective behavior of pupils. With respect to youngsters' cognitive gains, I have for years lauded the virtues of criterion-referenced rather than norm-referenced measures.[1]

There are two sorts of cognitive tests I'd like to see used in this evaluation. First, there would be a measure of the students' communication skills in writing and reading. Let's refer to this assessment device as the *Communication Skills Achievement Test*. Second, there would be a measure of the particular knowledge emphasized in the humanities program: for example, the elements and principles present in various art forms. Let's refer to this assessment device as the *Humanities Achievement Test*. These tests could either be developed locally if sufficient resources and expertise exist, or purchased from commercial firms if tests are found whose emphases mesh with those of the Radnor curriculum.

In addition, a comprehensive evaluation of the humanities program would definitely require the use of affective assessment devices—to get at such outcomes as "aesthetic sensibility" and an appreciation of human achievement in the arts.

Since these kinds of affective measures aren't currently sitting on test publishers' shelves, their creation would be a job for the educational evaluator. When using affective measures for purposes of program evalua-

---

[1] See, for example, *Modern Educational Measurement* (Englewood Cliffs, N.J.: Prentice-Hall, 1981), which not only deals adroitly with this point, but with every other worthwhile topic in the field of educational measurement. (This objective book review is supplied without charge by your nonpartisan author.)

tion, it is *not* necessary for those measures to yield responses valid for *individual* pupils. Instead, it is quite sufficient for such instruments to yield data that *in the aggregate* permit the drawing of valid inferences about the affective status of a group of pupils. What we want here is an idea of the affective status of approximately 800 sixth, seventh, and eighth grade students at Radnor Middle School *as a group*.[2]

Although our technical sophistication in this aspect of program evaluation is far from sufficient, we do possess some reasonably decent schemes for constructing valid and reliable affective assessment instruments. If I were carrying out this evaluation, I would work closely with the four members of the humanities department, since it would be imperative to secure their approval of the instruments I'd be creating. I would attempt to build one or more devices, typically relying on anonymous self-report instruments for each of the major noncognitive objectives of the program.

Another sort of information I'd want to bring to the attention of the decision makers would be cost data. I would want any cost savings associated with closing down the humanities program to be evident to the board. Since all four of the program's teachers are certified to teach in other departments (three in English and one in music), there would be no instant firings. I would portray the cost data, however, in an *opportunity cost* framework so that board members could see what benefits they are giving up by continuing the program. I'd like them to see how much additional instructional time might be devoted to other subjects if the demise of the humanities program resulted in availability of two more classes per week.

Finally, I'd gather some information about potential unanticipated effects, either positive or negative, from the students who are experiencing the humanities program. I'd rely on open-ended questionnaires and interviews consisting of a few questions such as "What were the best (worst) effects of the humanities program for you personally?"

Gathering the Goodies

Thus far I've isolated four sorts of data: (1) student performance on two cognitive tests, (2) student performance on various affective measures, (3) opportunity cost information, and (4) student reactions to open-ended questionnaires and interviews. How should we gather these data?

---

[2] For an absolutely enthralling discussion of this point, see the chapter on affective assessment in a scintillating text by W. James Popham, *Criterion-Referenced Measurement* (Englewood Cliffs, N.J.: Prentice-Hall, 1978).

It is important to note that there is only one middle school in the Radnor Township district, and all students in that school are enrolled in the humanities program. The possibility thus disappears of using any laboratory-derived data-gathering designs that assign students randomly to treatment and nontreatment conditions.

There are, however, comparable middle schools in nearby districts where no required humanities curriculum exists. If it makes sense to compare Radnor's pupils and other "untreated" pupils, we could set up a *nonequivalent control group design* to contrast the performance of differently treated but somewhat comparable groups.

I would recommend use of such a design for all affective measures and for the *Humanities Achievement Test*. These instruments would be administered at each grade level near the close of the academic year in the Radnor Middle School and, hopefully, two or more comparable schools. To reduce the assessment time in Radnor and elsewhere, we would sample up a storm. It's not necessary to drink an entire quart of milk to find out whether it's sour or sweet.

If it were accompanied by some comparative data, I would not administer the *Communication Skills Achievement Test* to students in other schools. We could see how Radnor's pupils stacked up on writing and reading by contrasting their scores with those in the norm group. If no comparative data were available, then I'd also administer that test to a small sample of youngsters in nearby middle schools. Board members have a right to know how their middle school pupils compare with others regarding the mastery of basic skills.

The cost data and open-ended data I'd gather only in Radnor, since contrasts with other situations would not be all that meaningful. Finally, I'd array all these data in several easy-to-understand charts, such as bar graphs. I would assiduously eschew complex statistical presentations (even though I once wrote a statistical book and could now toss in another unbiased footnote).

Wrinkle Time

To get a firm fix on the board's likely satisfaction with my report, I would prepare in advance of data collection a *mock evaluation report* presenting admittedly fictitious data. Then I'd ask board members to see if there were omissions or redundancies in the content, structure, or style of the report. Such a mock evaluation report can prove heuristically helpful in such settings. I would certainly attend to the reactions of the board members, modifying my evaluation plans as appropriate.

I'd keep the report itself as brief as possible. I am a solid proponent of a less-is-more approach; evaluation reports should not be tomes, they should be teensies.

I'd circulate the final report in draft form to those individuals most concerned with the program, that is, the humanities department faculty and Principal Janson. I would take seriously their criticisms. If it were forthcoming, I would wallow in any praise.

There are scores of evaluation nuances that space prohibitions preclude my mentioning. For instance, I've learned via a score of hard-knock experiences that the quality of interpersonal relationships between evaluator, evaluatee, and decision makers is crucial. I'd work darned hard to establish relationships of trust between me and the other parties in the endeavor.

I'd also rely heavily on the students themselves. We are dealing here with young people whose blossoming maturity may put them in a very special position to appraise what's going on in the humanities program. I'd seek their advice frequently as I went about my instrument design and data-gathering.

But enough of these subtleties. I've set out the major ingredients in my approach to the evaluation of Radnor's humanities program. A decent evaluative job would cost a fair amount of money, because we're talking about getting a fix on some rather elusive outcomes. To get first-rate evaluators to spend a lot of time in the Radnor Township Schools—well, that would be difficult unless you paid them well. Now, if you want me to evaluate the humanities program in the Maui Middle School, I'd take on that assignment for a few pineapples and, of course, travel expenses.

2.
Five Phases of Purposeful Inquiry

by Deborah G. Bonnet

Deborah Bonnet has been especially active in evaluation, having conducted over 25 evaluations of educational programs. She is a practitioner whose experience has come from "out there in the trenches." Bonnet is Director, Research and Evaluation Programs, New Educational Directions, Inc., Crawfordsville, Indiana.

To Evaluate or Not To Evaluate?

Before accepting an assignment to evaluate the Radnor humanities program, I would need some assurance that the school board really wanted it evaluated.

I'd begin with a long talk with the person who invited me into this battle: Radnor's principal, Anne Janson. Her advocacy of the humanities program is strong and public. Her goal is to preserve the program, and so far she has succeeded.

So why did she call me in? Why isn't she out celebrating her victory instead? If she leaves it alone, it may blow over, so why stir things up?

Her answer is that the program's reprieve is only temporary. Enrollments are still declining, the back-to-basics camp is still alive and well, and the humanities course is sure to be nominated as a victim of the next program cutbacks. That could happen at any time. When it does, she wants to be armed with a stack of data to prove the course's necessity.

That's reason enough to subject the program to further study. But is another public evaluation really in order?

The safest path to the goal of program preservation would be to take advantage of the calm after the storm. This time could be used to begin quietly compiling data to strengthen the program's defense. Asking too many people too many questions might just revive the controversy and

9

force the board to reconsider its decision to keep the program alive. Involving its opponents in another evaluation—or even letting them know that research is under way—would do the same.

In short, it may be in the program's best interests for the principal to do the study herself. I would advise her against attempting to be impartial. Even if she succeeded, it's unlikely that she'd convince the program's opposition of that. As long as her findings are represented as discrete pieces of evidence to substantiate her clear and open stance in favor of the program, she could skirt the ethical responsibilities that claims of an objective evaluation bring. Whether she should use public resources, even her own work time, for a secret pursuit of her personal goal is something else to consider.

I would go on to explain how things will go if she chooses instead to commission me to evaluate the program. My role as an independent evaluator would assume precedence over my current role as her personal advisor. I could not share her goal of preserving the humanities program. My mission would not be to advocate the program, but to bring the controversy to an equitable settlement. An impartial third party stance would be the most effective one for me to take.

Expediency aside, this role poses a dilemma for me. The problem is that my current thinking is *not* impartial. The program sounds wonderful to me; on paper, at least, it appeals to my views of what education ought to be: today's facts may be tomorrow's trivia; middle school should be exploratory as well as preparatory; education should develop every child's capacity for critical thinking; human experience is not compartmentalized into academic disciplines; students need to understand that it all fits together. All great concepts.

Then how would I manage to be impartial? First, I would employ the strategies anyone else would use to be objective—seek reliable information, distinguish between the relevant and the incidental, consider all sides of the issues, withhold final judgment until the data are in, and so forth. Second, I would arrange for someone else to monitor my execution of these vows—more on this later.

Finally, I would remind myself and others that the end product of the study will not be facts and figures, but eVALUations—that is, value judgments of whether the program should be continued. My evaluation of the program certainly will be shaped by my values, but it will not be *my* evaluation that decides whether the program stays or goes. Its fate will be determined through the school system's curriculum-setting process, which concludes with a school board decision. My role would be to facilitate rational decision making by those involved in each step of this process.

Rational evaluative decisions are made by integrating relevant information with values. My goal, then, would be to provide the right information to the right people in the right ways to enable them to reach the right decision about the program. The "right" decision is the one that is most compatible with the facts of the program and the values of the community.[1]

This means that I would have to (1) find out who in the community, besides the school board, influences curriculum decisions; (2) identify the values they will employ in evaluating the program; (3) collect data pertinent to those values; and (4) present the findings in a way that demonstrates their relevance to the humanities program debate.

My approach would make this evaluation at least as visible as the local review group's. We'll assume that the principal decides to risk the consequences (or that the decision is not hers to make).

The next question would be when to start. From a technical standpoint, it would be best to begin as soon as possible and finish as late as possible; as an evaluation timeline lengthens, the methodological options multiply. Under the circumstances, though, I'd recommend a starting date that balances the need for quick feedback with the need for enough time to work out the bugs in the newly-revised curriculum before subjecting it to critical review. The study should be concluded swiftly to avoid prolonging the agony, but not so hastily as to restrict the evaluation's scope to the trivial or its findings to the equivocal.

Then there would be contractual matters to negotiate. Besides the usual deliverables, deadlines, and terms of payment, the evaluation contract would stipulate agreements about access to data, protection of confidentiality, editorial privileges, dissemination of findings, acceptable reasons for contract termination, and procedures for amending the contract as the evaluation plan develops.

At this point I've established that an independent evaluation is desirable and that I am qualified to do it. I've determined its primary goal, clarified my role as an evaluation specialist, and reached formal agreements to ensure the study's effectiveness and integrity. Now it's time to get on with the evaluation itself. In this case, the steps would be to:

1. Learn more about the program and the setting.

2. Identify decision makers and their perspectives.

---

[1] At least, this is how *my* values say public school curriculum decisions should be made, which goes to show that the evaluation specialist's values are always a factor. Whether an evaluation is subjective or objective is not so much the question as whether the evaluator's values are introduced openly or subtly.

3. List all of the purposes, audiences, and questions the study might reasonably address.
4. Outline various methods for answering the proposed questions.
5. Decide which questions to pursue.
6. Complete the evaluation plan.
7. Collect and analyze data.
8. Report the findings.

Learn More About the Program and the Setting

Among my first questions about the humanities program would be: How long has it been around? How many and what kinds of students participate? What is the official curriculum? How is the program scheduled, staffed, funded, and coordinated? What other courses does the school offer? What are the district's grading system and testing program? What is the administrative structure of the district, is the school board elected or appointed, and how active is the PTA? What are the demographics of the district in general and the school's attendance zone in particular? Are there any local policies or state laws that might pertain to the program or the evaluation?

Most of this I could get from the principal, or whoever is designated as my primary contact. She would probably refer me to some documents to supplement the Humanities Curriculum Review Committee report—curriculm materials, the school schedule, policy statements, census data, and such.

Next I'd spend a few days wandering around the school. Most of the time I would spend in the humanities department getting acquainted with the students and teachers, developing a sense of the classroom atmosphere, observing how the curriculum is translated into classroom practice, and browsing through materials.

I'd ask to be introduced to the faculty or at least to the department heads. Stressing that my job is to study the humanities program, not to evaluate the staff, would be high on my agenda. My accessibility would be demonstrated through frequent visits to the faculty lounge, where I would also notice topics of conversation and staff relations. I might even suffer through school lunches and brave the hallways between class periods to observe how people behave and interact—to acquire a sense of the school's personality. After school I'd tour the town and read the local newspaper.

All of this would give me some hunches about the program and enough basic knowledge and vocabulary to discuss it intelligently with other outside observers.

Identify Decision Makers and Their Perspectives

Next would come finding out who will influence the program's fate, what they think about it, and what more they need to know.

First I'd look into what had already happened with the program. Why was it instituted? Why was it questioned? Why was it continued? Minutes of study committee and board meetings supplemented by interviews with the principal and review committee chair would be a start, but I might have to pursue other sources before feeling satisfied with my understanding of the debate.

To find out where the controversy stands and where it might go, I'd do a series of interviews starting with the superintendent and school board president. They would be loosely structured and aimed at discovering the individual's:

1. Current thinking on whether the program should be continued;

2. Perspectives on the program's strengths and weaknesses;

3. Criteria for evaluating the program, including (a) who else's opinion influences his or her own, (b) what new information about the program would sway his or her current position, and (c) what potential changes in the program would make it more or less acceptable; and

4. Concerns about other school issues.

In the first several interviews, I would also ask about plans for the process to re-evaluate the program's continuation and get advice about selecting other interviewees who might play key roles in the process. The final list of interviewees might include:

- All school board members
- The Radnor School principal
- The Humanities Curriculum Review Committee
- The humanities staff
- Other faculty leaders at Radnor School
- Central administrators with curricular influence
- The principal and humanities faculty of the high school where the students will go when they leave Radnor School
- The principals of the elementary schools where Radnor students come from
- Radnor School students
- High school students who took the humanities course
- Radnor School parent leaders
- Elementary and high school parent leaders
- Leaders in the community at large

All of these groups are potential "audiences" of the evaluation because they all have a stake in the program—and possibly a voice in deciding its future. Chances are that the evaluation budget and timeline wouldn't accommodate assessing, and later fulfilling, the information needs of every potential audience. So I'd limit myself to those whose voices are likely to be heard the loudest.

List All Possible Purposes, Audiences, and Questions

Then I'd go back home and spend several days sorting out what I had learned. I might diagram the power forces I expected to enter into the humanities decision. Even though this would never leave my office unless it matched official policy, it would underlie my recommendations about which audience's information needs should be given priority.

Although the evaluation's primary purpose—to facilitate the decision of whether to continue the humanities program—is already established, I'd think about other uses the study might serve. An obvious possibility is to propose compromises between the program's opponents and proponents, but there may be others.

Next I would generate a list of issues that might bear on the program's future; one column for propositions supporting the program and one for those against it. I would not be surprised to find some propositions in both columns. How many people mentioned each issue would be of little concern, but I would keep track of which audiences showed interest in each item on the list.

Most of the propositions would come directly from my interview notes, but some would be my own. Mine would be formulated on the basis of:

- Personal hypotheses regarding the program's strengths, weaknesses, and side effects;
- Discrepancies among interviewees' comments that had not been recognized as issues;
- Questionable assumptions underlying interviewees' remarks;
- Possibilities for the program to either provoke or alleviate other school problems;
- Any other factors I think should enter into the decision, even though nobody else had considered them.

The list might include some of the propositions in Figure 1.

The propositions would be translated into potential "evaluation questions." Evaluation questions are to evaluations what program objectives are to programs.

Figure 1. Issues Bearing on the Program's Future

Propositions For	Propositions Against

Curriculum

Propositions For	Propositions Against
• It's what middle school students need: opportunities to explore, create, synthesize, and so on. • It teaches acceptance of diverse value systems.	• Middle school students need other things more: work on basic language skills and social studies facts, for example. • It teaches acceptance of diverse value systems. • It teaches values contrary to our religious beliefs. • It embarrasses parents because they can't help their children with their homework.

Curriculum Implementation

Propositions For	Propositions Against
• The new curriculum is being implemented with fidelity and skill.	• The new curriculum is on paper only; the program hasn't changed. • Grading standards are too low.

Student Impact

Propositions For	Propositions Against
• Students learn to think critically. • It enhances students' self-esteem. • It helps students achieve in high school. • It reduces teenage sex and drug use. • It's effective for nearly everyone.	• Students fall behind in basic skills. • It hurts students' high school achievement. • It increases teenage sex and drug use. • It's ineffective for some types of students.

School Impact

Propositions For	Propositions Against
• It enhances students' aesthetic appreciation, thereby reducing school vandalism.	• It encourages students' "self-expression," thereby increasing discipline problems.

Propositions For	Propositions Against

Cost

• The declining enrollment problem could be solved without tampering with the humanities program.	• Eliminating it would save $100,000 per year.
• We could salvage the curriculum and reduce the school budget through reassignments.	

Audience Support

• Students (parents, the faculty, and others) are for it.	• Students (parents, the faculty, and others) are against it.

There are two reasons for restating propositions as questions: (1) to neutralize the evaluation's tone and (2) to tie together issues appearing in both the for and against column as contradictory claims. For example, the propositions that the humanities program contributes to achievement in high school and that it hinders it would become the question, "How does the humanities program affect students' achievement in high school?"

Outline Methods for Answering Questions

Next I would take each potential evaluation question and develop a rough plan for answering it. At the same time I would estimate the cost of implementing the plan and consider how definitive the answer is likely to be. For some questions I'd come up with several approaches; the next step might involve choosing the most feasible alternative. Or, if the question is especially important, I might approach it from several angles to increase the certainty of the answer.

By now it would surely have been pointed out to me that the program's fate cannot be decided in isolation. If it's dropped, something else will have to take place during those four hours per week in each student's schedule. This realization changes many of the evaluation questions from absolute ones (How good is the program?) to comparative ones (How good is the program compared to what would replace it?). In exploring the program and people's perspective of it, I would have learned what proposals are under consideration for replacing or revising it, and perhaps developed some proposals of my own. To the extent possible, I would have investigated the evaluation audiences' positions on these proposals.

I would also have checked the feasibility of various evaluation designs by finding out about the district's organization, identifying available data, sensing the acceptability of various data collection procedures, and noting the credibility of different kinds of data with various audiences.

For the sake of simplicity, we'll assume the curriculum of a middle school in a nearby district is the most likely alternative to the Radnor humanities program. We'll further assume that the other middle school, which we'll call the comparison school, serves a similar population and feeds into a similar high school. This is a naively optimistic set of assumptions, but we'll make them anyway to avoid dwelling on the technicalities of evaluation design. Less ideal circumstances would restrict options somewhat, but many of the problems could be skirted by using historical data or going elsewhere for comparison purposes.

Evaluation methodologies would follow directly from the evaluation questions actually being considered at this point, but here are some thoughts on addressing the issues shown in Figure 1.

Curriculum Issues

Having the review committee of parents and educators analyze the curriculum was a good idea. Educators in general and evaluators in particular often get so caught up with what students are actually learning that we forget to look at what they are being given an *opportunity* to learn. The earlier analysis appears thorough and does not need repeating, but submitting the curriculum to other authorities might serve a purpose. Several child development experts representing different schools of thought could respond to charges that students of this age need something else more than they need humanities. Their analysis of the course would have to be within the context of the total school curriculum. Leaders representing the community's predominant religions could be invited to comment on the curriculum's compatibility with the tenets of their faiths. That could get interesting.

Curriculum Implementation

Analyses of instructional materials and lesson plans, teacher and student interviews, and classroom observations could address the fidelity and quality of implementation of the revised curriculum. The charge that grading standards are too low could be checked by analyzing the standards and comparing students' grades in this course to those they receive in others.

Student and School Impact

I would not reject the possibility of locating or even creating measures of the program's student learning objectives, slippery though they are. I doubt, though, that evaluating achievement of the program's controversial objectives would make them any less controversial.

My guess is that subjecting the program to more conservative criteria of educational value would be more effective in settling the dispute. Standardized tests of basic skills could be used to respond to the concern that the humanities program causes students to fall behind. Scores made by Radnor students could be compared with those from the comparison school. An alternative would be to compare Radnor eighth-graders' reading and language arts norm-referenced achievement scores with (a) their math scores, (b) their aptitude scores, or (c) their fifth-grade reading and language arts scores.

For all their faults as achievement measures, grades in high school are meaningful to the public. Former Radnor students' grades could be compared to those of the comparison school's graduates; other comparisons of the two schools' graduates might deal with their high school course selections, involvement in extra-curricular activities, and drop-out rates. The drawback of the follow-up approach is that it would address effectiveness of the *old* humanities program—or it would delay that part of the evaluation for several years.

Other criteria of student and school impact that might or might not respond to questions people are actually asking include criterion-referenced test performance, attendance rates, disciplinary incidents, school vandalism, and drug problems.

Since the earlier review group's conclusion that humanities should be required is still at issue, an analysis of the course's differential effects on students with various characteristics would probably be in order. Measures of student impact would have to be analyzed to check whether the program was ineffective or harmful for certain youngsters. If so, further analyses would attempt to identify common characteristics of those students. These findings would be useful in placement decisions if the program became elective.

Cost

The program's cost is sure to be an issue. I might begin by calculating a total that would include a portion of the school's noninstructional expenses, as well as the direct costs of the humanities staff, materials, and equipment. I would definitely not stop there; this figure could too easily be misconstrued as the amount that would be saved by eliminating the program. Much more relevant is the effect on the total school budget of adopting various replacements for the program or revisions of it.

If my earlier investigation revealed cost as a major issue, the evaluation's central focus would be on identifying cost-saving alternatives, studying the feasibility of adopting them, and estimating the impact of doing so. In this case, cost analyses would come first. Only modifications of and substitutes for humanities that would result in significant savings would warrant further comparisons to the current program's merits.

Audience Support

Since their constituencies' opinions of humanities are likely to influence the final decision makers' positions, an opinion poll might be in order. However, I would delay it until the other evaluation results were announced or make it the kind that asks, "If the evaluation results showed X, then what would you think?" More on this in a moment.

Decide Which Questions to Answer

Now I would have a list of possible evaluation questions and a menu of evaluation methods whose costs total four or five times the evaluation budget. The next task would be to pare the list down to something affordable.

I wouldn't do it myself. This is the single most important decision point in the study and an excellent opportunity to introduce my biases. All I'd have to do to make the program look good is to collect the information most likely to turn program opponents into proponents without alienating its current supporters.

One way to keep the competition fair would be to establish an evaluation steering committee. I would recommend including representatives of various audiences such as students, faculty, administration, parents, and the school board, but more important than that would be getting an equal number of members who support and oppose the program.

I'd give them my lecture about the important role of evaluation questions and how they should be selected according to:

(1) The *value* of having the answer. In this case, the most valuable answers would be the ones most likely to influence the positions of those with the most control over the program's future.

(2) The *cost* of getting the answer, which should never exceed the value of having it. Program disruption as well as direct evaluation costs should be considered.

(3) How *definitive* the answer is likely to be. For example, the answer to, "How many students got A's in humanities last semester?" should be straight and precise. The one to, "What does the course do for youngsters' aesthetic sensibilities?" would probably be neither.

Then I'd brief the steering committee on which audiences had indicated interest in which issues and share my speculations about which questions would be most influential.

I'd remind them that my interview samples were selected to uncover the widest possible range of perspectives, not to measure their pervasiveness. Then I'd ask the committee if they wanted me to conduct formal polls of any of the audiences to get an accurate reading of how different evaluation findings would affect the groups' positions on humanities. One finding from such a poll might be:

> "Evidence that humanities students do not fall behind on basic skills would increase parent support from 52 percent to 71 percent. Even slight indications that they *do* fall behind would reduce parent support to 28 percent."

These data would not only guide decisions about what data to collect; they would also tell the school board how to evaluate the final results of the study to reflect their constituents' values. This might be more help in the decision-making process than the board would want from me.

Whether or not the poll idea went through, it would be up to the steering committee to tell me which evaluation questions to pursue. Each question would have a price tag, so I might split the budget in two and let each subcommittee—the "pros" and the "cons"—decide how to invest their half in building their case. It would be up to them to work out the negotiations for questions that could turn out to support either side.

Complete the Evaluation Plan

This would be a matter of putting together the separate plans for the questions selected for study and working out the details. The products of this task would include a timeline, a staffing plan, data collection instruments and procedures, sampling plans, data analysis plans, and reporting specifications. It would be subject to the steering committee's approval. I would particularly call their attention to potential sources of bias, such as:

• Questionnaires and interview guides, whose questions might be slanted to favor or discredit humanities;

• Tests and other measures of student learning, whose content might match one curriculum better than another in unintended ways; and

• Selection of other evaluators, such as the clergy, to review the curriculum and of observers to assess its implementation.

Collect and Analyze Data

These steps usually overlap with the last one. My general rule of evaluation planning is to think ahead, but to postpone final decisions until the last possible moment. This way, the evaluation can build on preliminary findings.

Say, for example, that a new proposal for a humanities replacement comes up halfway through the evaluation—or that a child development authority who reviews the curriculum proposes a theory that should predict which students will benefit from the humanities program and which would be better off elsewhere. It would be unfortunate if the evaluation lacked the flexibility to follow through on these developments.

Report the Findings

My first progress report would be to the school board and perhaps to the press at the point when the evaluation questions were chosen. Unless there were a possibility that later findings would shed a different light on them, I would release early findings while the study was still in progress if they could be put to immediate use or if it would stimulate healthy interest in the final report.

There would be at least three written final reports. One would be a full technical report; although I'd make every effort to make it interesting, I wouldn't expect more than a handful of people to read it. Another would be ten or fifteen pages giving the findings in some detail, and mentioning just enough about methods to give the study credibility. The third would be only a page or two. All three reports would be easily accessible to the public, as stipulated in my contract some months ago. The evaluation steering committee would review and comment on the drafts but I would hold final editorial authority.

The reports would be organized around the evaluation questions: first the questions, then the short answers, then the substantiating evidence and qualifications. They would conclude with summaries of arguments for continuing the humanities program in its current form and for adopting various alternatives. In this particular case I would probably refrain from presenting my own recommendations in writing, but I would give them orally if asked.

Soon after release of the written reports, there would be a series of oral presentations to assemblies of the evaluation's audiences—the administration, the humanities staff, the Radnor School faculty, the PTA, the student government, and the local press are all likely candidates. I'd ask the steering committee to come along; perhaps we would stage debates, with me moderating citations of the findings. If the school board would stand for it, some or all of these sessions would conclude with an audience survey—essentially a vote—on what to do with the program.

I'd meet with the school board members, either in an executive session or individually, in advance of the public meeting. The superintendent might choose to accompany me but I'd leave the steering committee home. The results of any post-evaluation opinion surveys would be delivered to the board at this time and we'd talk about my role on the big night. I'd be bargaining for a final showing of the debate-report, complete with steering committee and audience participation.

My work would end just as it began: with a long talk with the principal. This time she'd get my congratulations or condolences along with whatever advice I could offer on her next challenge—to execute the board's decision with authority and grace.

In General

Every productive evaluation is unique. Every program has its own features and circumstances calling for its own evaluative approach. To illustrate, these are among the factors that shaped my proposal for evaluating the humanities program: The evaluation's goal is clear and summative. The program is the object of a heated public dispute, and the issues are complex and value-laden. The program's objectives are difficult to measure, but whether they are achieved is less at issue than whether they are *worth* achieving. Whether they are worth achieving is less at issue than what else may be *more* worth achieving. The declining enrollment crisis demands austerity. Austerity demands choices, priorities, painful examination of values. The thought that went into the first humanities program evaluation and the suffering that went into the resulting decision show that the community is taking its new challenge seriously.

But even if I'd been asked to evaluate an obscure new program with simple objectives—even if it were statewide or national, and even if a regulation rather than an identified need prompted the study—I would proceed in much the same way.

I see evaluations as having five phases: (1) obligation, (2) exploration, (3) design, (4) execution, and (5) application. Evaluations often cycle through all or some of the phases several times. In fact, it is best when they do; each cycle can build on the findings from the previous one. Here is what happens in each phase and how it relates to the humanities plan:

1. Obligation

The products of this phase are the agreement to conduct an evaluation and the ground rules for doing so. The tasks are to:

a. Verify that the climate is amenable to the ethical conduct of an evaluation with a reasonable likelihood of effecting a desirable impact.

b. Set the evaluation's overall goal and boundaries.

c. Establish the roles of evaluation specialists and other participants in the study.

d. Reach agreements with the evaluation's commissioners on the handling of potential threats to the study's feasibility, accuracy, propriety, and utility.

In the humanities program's case, this phase would consist of an examination of the study committee report, my initial discussions with the principal, and contract negotiations.

2. Exploration

The main product of this phase is an understanding of the evaluation's context and potential accomplishments.

a. Collect basic facts about the program and its setting: history, official goals, administrative structure, and so on.

b. Develop a tentative sense of the character of the program and environment: distinctive features, human interactions, operational goals, possible side-effects, and so forth.

c. Probe the perspectives of other observers and participants.

d. Analyze the program as a system and as a part of other systems.

e. List salient features, issues, discrepancies.

f. List all the purposes, audiences, and questions the evaluation might address.

g. Identify factors affecting the feasibility of various data collection and reporting options.

In the humanities program, the tasks labeled "learn more about the program and the setting," "identify decision makers and their perspectives," and "list all possible purposes, audiences, and questions," fall into this phase. However, exploration would continue through the aftermath of the final report even though more visible activities were underway.

3. Design

The products of the design phase are plans for data collection, analyses, and reporting. This and the next phase are often repeated several times during the course of an evaluation. In fact, "exploration" is essentially the first cycle of phases 3 and 4.

    a. Set priorities for potential purposes and audiences.

    b. Outline possible methods for each proposed question.

    c. Estimate the cost and feasibility of each method.

    d. Predict the validity of the findings from each method.

    e. Decide which questions to pursue and which methods to use.

    f. Integrate the selected methods into a cohesive plan.

    g. Develop the plan into specific tools and procedures—develop or choose instruments, select samples and software packages, and so on.

    h. Develop specifications for the audiences, contents, and formats of evaluation reports.

"Outline methods," "decide which questions to answer," and "complete the evaluation plan" discuss these tasks for the humanities program.

4. Execution

The products of this phase are written evaluation reports. The tasks are to:

    a. Collect data

    b. Analyze data

    c. Write evaluation reports

These activities vary from the mechanical to the artistic, depending on what information is collected, how liberally it is interpreted, and how creatively it is presented. "Collect and analyze data" and the first part of "report findings" are in this phase.

5. Application

The product here is the evaluation's impact. If all goes well, this includes new insights, rational decisions, program improvements, and freshly motivated staff. The evaluation specialist's part is to:

    a. Produce sound information in response to real information needs.

    b. Report the findings in ways that are understandable, credible, and palatable to the evaluation's audiences.

    c. Ensure that the audiences have access to the findings and aggressively encourage them to use them.

    d. Venture beyond the findings themselves to what should be done about them, or lead the evaluation audiences in doing this for themselves.

    That's the evaluator's part. The rest of the job of making evaluations effective is up to the people who run the schools.

3.
Evaluating Responsively

by Robert E. Stake and James A. Pearsol

Robert Stake was trained in rigorous, empirical methods but now prefers a more descriptive approach, exemplified by a series of case studies he edited with Jack Easley for the National Science Foundation in 1978. He and James Pearsol offer a narrative account of their imaginary evaluation in order to show how one event leads to another in responsive evaluation. Stake is Professor of Educational Psychology, University of Illinois, and Director of the Center for Instructional Research and Curriculum Evaluation, Urbana, Illinois. James Pearsol is a graduate student in educational psychology at the University of Illinois, and a co-author of several works on vocational planning and education.

"But you have not evaluated this program!" charged the president of the board of education. She was speaking to the Humanities Curriculum Review Committee—eleven educators and six parents. They had spent several months reviewing the Radnor School humanities program and recommended that it be continued with some modification. Members of the board felt the committee's report did not constitute an "evaluation" of the humanities curriculum. More information was needed. What is the impact on students? Is the course too "advanced" for middle school students? How might the program be scheduled and staffed in light of declining enrollment?

The Center for Instructional Research and Curriculum Evaluation (CIRCE) was awarded a personal services contract of $500 to evaluate the program. Jim Pearsol, a doctoral student in educational psychology and program evaluation, volunteered his free, part-time services. His evaluation professor, Bob Stake, was happy to give him advice.

Negotiating the Design

Jim arranged to meet with Principal Anne Janson and the school board at their January meeting. Although the board, by majority vote,

25

had approved continuation of the humanities program, they expressed great interest in what an evaluation study would show. They particularly stressed the need for information on program effectiveness for future planning in the face of a shrinking budget. At the meeting, the principal reiterated an earlier claim that effectiveness could not be measured statistically; for example, by analysis of test scores. She added that many outcomes of the humanities curriculum should be characterized as "experimental enrichment" and "personal interpretation," rather than "achievement of common objectives or competencies."

Jim asked if the evaluation should confine itself to the board's questions or whether it could consider questions raised by others. He was told to evaluate broadly—as long as the board's questions were answered.

He explained to the board that he had approximately three weeks to devote to the project. He could arrange his time flexibly, but preferred to spend a few days a month, across four months. The board then asked how he might address their primary concerns.

Jim suggested focusing first on one or two main issues, understanding that the evaluation might later produce additional issues worthy of investigation. The board agreed. They selected *impact on students* as the most important concern. Jim suggested the evaluation might consider "opportunity costs"—what other learnings or student experiences are overshadowed or ignored by continuing the humanities program. This too met with board approval.

Mrs. Janson then asked, "How are you going to gather information and how will students, faculty, and others be involved?"

Jim said that in six weeks he would present to the board some portrayals of student experience. These should indicate program impact in broader terms than standardized test scores. He discouraged the idea of trying to measure the same achievement on each student, saying:

"Suppose we were to determine some behavioral objective and measure it. For instance, 'the student will read an article about the elderly in colonial America and write a two-page paper, without punctuation errors, describing colonial-era perceptions of the elderly.' What does that tell us about the impact of the assignment on the students? Is 'impact' simply the ability to produce a paper without punctuation errors? Or is it that these historical perceptions might help students shape or question their own perceptions of the elderly? Our tests and scales are not sensitive to such 'measurement' criteria.

"Students get different understandings from a course. Consider your unit on 'Masks and Sculptures,' emphasizing work that reflects an artist's culture. Some students may appreciate a mask as a piece of art representing human expression common to all cultures. Other students may come to understand the same object within the specific cultural context, such as recognizing the function of a mask in telling a story. One understanding is not more 'right' than another. It is difficult to test for individualistic understandings. We need to study some student impact in the context of each student's personal experiences.

"Finally, it would be worthwhile to contrast reported student activity with observations of classroom interaction. That is, do humanities teachers encourage disciplined reflection by students? Do the goals and objectives outlined in the curriculum report get translated into experience? These are dimensions within which we might assess student impact."

In terms of faculty, student, and others' involvement, Jim requested that he have full access to the faculty and students in the program for interviews and classroom observations. He would alert faculty members to his visits and arrange mutually acceptable times for discussions and observations. He expected to preserve the confidentiality of data collected. To accomplish this, he would not quote any individual in his report unless he had the person's permission. In situations where classroom interactions were observed, he would get permission or use fictitious names. Finally, he proposed showing the final evaluation report to the principal and board before release, but they would not have veto authority. Mrs. Janson immediately interjected, "I'm not sure that's fair to the teachers and students involved."

Jim responded that the preliminary review by board and principal would be helpful in correcting factual errors, but he felt that to preserve the integrity of the results he would have to be assured final authority on changes. A board member said, "Why doesn't our principal write a 'minority opinion' if there is some disagreement over the results?" Jim liked the idea. Mrs. Janson agreed, too, but added that the teachers should be asked rather than required to participate.

The meeting ended with the following plan of action. Jim would spend another day at the school to review the curriculum study report, class texts, and lesson plans; to talk with the humanities faculty; and to gather additional information about the program. He would then return to CIRCE and prepare a calendar of activities and a list of questions to guide his observations and study.

Recording the Evolution of Issues

Back home, Jim and Bob made a list of "foreshadowing" questions:

1. What are the justifications for this humanities curriculum?
2. What are the students getting out of it?

3. What is the history of its development here?

4. How is instruction different in the humanities courses from other courses at Radnor School?

5. Why did the Humanities Curriculum Review Committee make such specific recommendations for assessing student progress?

When Principal Janson read the list and recalled the January board meeting, she added two more questions:

6. What levels of intellectual maturity are required of students here?

7. How does this sequence of courses escape the designation of "frill courses," which the superintendent pledged to eliminate?

Jim and Bob did not have answers to these questions, but used them as conceptual organizers in the initial phase of the evaluation study.

Jim reviewed the humanities curriculum committee report and talked with some of the humanities faculty about the program. They believed the *experience* of the humanities was the most important aspect of the program. They felt that the majority of the committee, including the parents, shared these views. In fact, parents in the Parent Teacher Organization had passed a resolution to endorse the goals and objectives listed in the committee report. They saw this as a way to legitimatize and protect the program's educational experiences.

Later, Jim talked with two English department faculty members, who seemed less enthusiastic. One said, "We really feel we need to sharpen academic standards. There seem to be very few writing or extended reading assignments in the humanities program. We feel that the humanities faculty are over there in their special program having lots to say about disciplined inquiry, thinking, and expression—but they have not articulated their performance standards."

Excerpts from the humanities committee's recommendations for increased written and oral assessments had also identified a need for specific performance standards. Although the total report highlighted the value of humanities *experiences* for middle school children, the guidelines left no doubt as to methods for assessing student progress (Appendix B, p. 113):

B. An increase in the number of formal writing assignments:
   1. Four formal writing assignments, written either in class or as homework, per pupil per trimester; each paper to be graded by the teacher, corrected by the student, signed by the parent, and kept on file with the teacher.
G. Increased number of objective tests, particularly in grades seven and eight.
H. Introduction of an A, B, C, D, U grading system to replace the E, S, U system currently in use.

When questioned on the telephone by Bob, one humanities faculty member said, "I really find it difficult to reach the goals of 'disciplined inquiry, thinking, and expression in written and oral forms.' In some respects, the new modifications and objectives—with their focus on increased testing, reading, and writing—further remove us from the opportunity to help students understand the humanities in the context of their own lives."

Other members of the humanities faculty spoke of difficulty in defining *in advance* the changes in students that would represent understanding of the humanities. They conceded that it was easy to test children on definitions of art or satire, but they wanted also to measure the degree to which students acquired personal insights.

Examining Student Impact

Jim decided it was time for him to concentrate on the students themselves. He chose several to observe closely. On each, he prepared a folder of anecdotes, hoping to show the humanities concepts and language they were acquiring. He checked with the people who knew these children to see how they were maturing intellectually. Attributing such gain to any particular lesson or course would be difficult, often impossible.

For instance, one humanities teacher pointed out Matthew, a sixth-grader. "He wouldn't do an oral report in class until we reached a unit on artistic style. Matthew brought in the album "Off the Wall" by Michael Jackson and told us about the artist's style and why he liked the music." Jim talked with Matthew.

Matthew: "The first thing we did in this class was a lesson on talking with other people . . . the ways we talk. Sometimes we talk by using words and sometimes by not using words."

Jim: "What are ways that people talk without words?"

Matthew: "Sign language, like if you can't hear . . . "

Jim: "How do *you* talk without words?"

Matthew: "I don't know. I guess I talk; I don't have to use sign language."

Then he talked about other lessons.

Matthew: "One day we had to look at pictures of buildings. It was no fun at all."

Jim: "Were you supposed to look for something special?"

Matthew: "I guess to see that buildings can be art."

He then used the word "architecture." Jim asked Matthew to tell him what architecture meant and to make up a sentence using the word.

Matthew said architecture meant "building," as in, "I live in an architecture on Front Street."

Matthew was able to frame classroom experiences with personal context. Occasionally his renditions showed his understandings to be unique or, in the case of "architecture," simply wrong.

Jim learned that Matthew and his Boy Scout troop had recently gone on a winter camping trip. Jim talked to the scoutmaster, who said Matthew had worried a lot about the youngest member of the troop, a boy who had never spent a night away from his family before.

For his geography class, Matthew was assigned to write about how farms are changing: "Long ago farmers had to be brave and daring. Today they have air-conditioned tractors."

Jim also found out that Matthew had argued with his friend Doyle about whether it was fair for the band leader to leave Doyle off the team for the regional music contest. Matthew took the position that it is necessary to have limits, but he seemed not to have a reason why.

Giving Interim Feedback

Jim used his student folders and several indications of group achievement in an interim report to the school board. He later met with a few members of the board, the principal, and a humanities teacher to discuss the student portrayals. Jim repeated some of his earlier remarks about the complexity of the learning process and the different understandings students acquire. He pointed out, using his folders, examples of convergence and divergence on the course objectives. He wanted to continue using individual student reports to describe the varieties of impact experienced by students in the program. Some board members expressed disappointment that the information on student impact was so "personalized" and "incomplete." Jim suggested that these portrayals might tell the board more about the experience of the program. He agreed there were incomplete features to the evaluation. He pointed out that more analytic and objective measures of student achievement were included in the trimester grade reports.

Jim referred to his evolving list of issues and got suggestions for further change in emphasis. More concern about the legitimacy of the program's objectives emerged. Jim next decided to go back to Radnor School and meet with teachers from other departments.

Getting Additional Information

Some teachers questioned any need for the humanities curriculum.

A social studies teacher said, "Sure, we're tied up with curriculum require-
ments, but I think having a separate humanities department takes some
of the glimmer out of our program." A biology teacher said, "I think
they're making a big deal out of nothing. They get two periods a week
to work on 'humanities.' What do you call English and social studies?"

There seemed to be a competitive feeling between the humanities
department and some of the other departments. Although most faculty
members spoke of the importance of the humanities, few endorsed the
program in its present form. Some felt the program detracted from other
humanities-related disciplines; some felt the standards were ill-defined;
some took exception to the attention focused on the program and its
special status. Some faculty saw the rewards for teaching in the school
largely focused on the humanities program.

Other faculty members complained of an elitist orientation in the
humanities department. Jim augmented his observations using two kinds
of interviews: (1) He taped humanities teachers talking about the differences among elitism, snobbery, and caring about aesthetic quality. (2) He
asked a student to keep a log on comments made in school about student
homelife.

Jim talked with some of the district central office staff about other
educational program possibilities for Radnor School. He asked about
specific programs that might be instituted both with and without the budget
commitment to the current humanities program. The central office staff
expressed surprise at the prospect of program options other than the
humanities curriculum. One staff member put it this way, "I'd like to see
us create a remedial reading lab instead, but with all this parent support
for the humanities program, it would be political suicide to cut the
program!"

The central office staff could identify program alternatives, but saw
little reason to introduce changes. Although there were expressions of
discontent, neither faculty nor central office staff members stepped forward
to propose changes in the humanities program.

Reporting the Evaluation Study

At the close of the evaluation work, the issue list was headed by four
matters: (1) concerns about assessing the experience of the humanities;
disagreements about (2) the need for the humanities curriculum and (3)
the form it should take; and (4) the absence of alternatives to the program. Several original issues had been left unattended. What features of
instruction differentiate the humanities from other courses at Radnor

School? What levels of intellectual maturity are required to assimilate the issues of the program? Should the humanities courses escape the superintendent's vow to eliminate "frill courses"? Jim felt the evaluation study was incomplete. With Bob, he spent considerable time trying to refute, add to, or expand these issues by rereading the curriculum committee report and his notes from interviews and observations. Jim asked himself, "Was my personal bias giving added weight to a particular point of view? Did I guide the interviews to a more positive or negative focus? Was any particular group's position ignored?"

Jim's task was now to report his collection of responses about the humanities program, which he portrayed through the experiences of the people involved. He conditioned his descriptions with understanding of what board members seemed to know about the school, its programs, its people, and about a humanities curriculum. First he described the program's operation. He used excerpts of observed interactions between humanities teachers and students, inserting quotes from students. He felt that vignettes showing events as they occurred would give readers of his report a sense of vicarious participation in the program.

Jim described the format and context of the program, making sure to report negative and positive comments about program organization. He introduced the predominant four issues, telling how they had emerged in his investigation.

He did not report student impact specifically in terms of test score means. Rather, he interspersed incidents of individual student experiences that showed the understandings they had acquired. He included samples of student writing, interview reports, observations, faculty assessments, scores on unit tests, and trimester grades. All of these served as records of student impact.

His final evaluation report was meant to capture the growing disillusionment, the hard work, the confusion, and the engaging qualities of the humanities program.

Although Jim's presence in some ways interrupted the normal flow of activities in Radnor School, the intent was to observe activity and setting, to record and question what he saw, to validate interpretations, to report the predominant issues, and to present all of this in the words and images of the people involved.

The steps of responsive evaluation here were:

- Negotiating with the sponsors a framework for the evaluation study
- Eliciting topics or questions of concern from the sponsors
- Formulating foreshadowing questions for initial guidance
- Entering the scene of the evaluation and observing it

- Paring down information, questioning it, identifying themes and issues
- Presenting these initial findings in an interim report
- Investigating more fully the predominant issues and concerns
- Looking for conflicting evidence that would invalidate findings
- Reporting the results in narrative style for the reader

Jim wondered if he had done too little to constitute an "evaluation study." He and Bob reviewed the possibilities for missed opportunities. First of all, the budget largely determined the sum of resources (for tests, consultants, and so on) at their disposal. Aside from that, they believed the situation to be evaluated was defined largely by the Radnor humanities program itself. They considered comparing the program to the elementary and high school programs there, but that seemed beyond the scope of the study. They might have asked, "What does the humanities currriculum specifically say about the educational practices of the school and the district?" But this also seemed beyond the scope of the study.

What Jim and Bob tried to accomplish was a review of the humanities curriculum as it was perceived by the key individuals associated with it. In its incompleteness, it seemed inappropriate to call the report a case study, although it had many features of a case study. By responding to the concerns of various "constituencies," they generated a responsive evaluation report.

4.
The Radnor Evaluation Derby

by Michael Scriven

Michael Scriven is the evaluator's philosopher, recognized for his original thinking on "goal-free evaluation" and his introduction of such terms as "summative" and "formative." Scriven was a mathematician before he took his doctorate in philosophy at Oxford and is no stranger to the humanities. As this chapter shows, he can be an outspoken dissenter. Scriven is the University Professor at the University of San Francisco.

Good evaluators should be very sensitive to the context in which an evaluation is to be designed or done. In this case there is a *simulated* context (Radnor) and an *actual* one (the ASCD project). My proposals are about the first context, but done in the second context, and are responsive to it. So the reader should not conclude that what I propose here is exactly what I would do at Radnor as a sole evaluator; it's what I *say* I'd do at Radnor, given that six other evaluators are addressing the same topic and will surely cover the conventional bases, and given that I'm *not* in fact hired at Radnor. This is either cheating or answering the precise question we were asked; the reader must decide (and will then be graded pass or fail by the Great Evaluator in the Sky).

The assignment was "to explain in a general way how . . . to evaluate" this program, that is, a design assignment. I am pleased to be able to do much more than this at no extra charge. This is a welcome contrast to the all-too-common situation in evaluation where we do much *less* than requested, *despite* an extra charge.

What I am prepared to do is not just the design but the actual evaluation; and to do this without further data-gathering, interviews, testing, background investigation, travel to the site, and so on. In the annals of evaluation, this is more or less the equivalent of the miracle of the loaves and fishes. Given that the total client cost (Radnor + ASCD) was zero, I am also nominating it for the Guinness Book of Records, Cost-Effective

34

Evaluation Division. To support that nomination, however, we first have to prove that the effects of the evaluation will be beneficial.

The Bottom Line

Let us begin at the end, to reduce the reader's anxiety, and reveal the bottom line of evaluation: *Abolish the program, as soon as possible, regardless of whether it is replaced by another "humanities" program, basics, or bicycle-riding.*

The legitimacy of drawing such a conclusion from purely documentary evidence is area-dependent. That is, one could not do it if the program were, for instance, in physical education or math. In such cases, no matter how poor the program rationales[1] provided by program faculty, one would have to investigate the possibility that their actual teaching, in the area of their professional competence, is much better than their capacity to write about the philosophy of the curriculum. But in this case, the program rationale *is* in the area of the faculty's professional competence, since it is a discussion about the nature and importance of the humanities in education, which is a crucial and not atypical topic in the humanities. Moreover, one can reasonably infer that it represents their best shot, since it was done in the context of a threat to their very survival. Since the program rationale is totally incompetent, as I shall illustrate below, we can reasonably infer that the faculty's *best* work is incompetent. And since it is easy, in the present market, to get competent teachers of the humanities, and of other subjects, we can hardly avoid the conclusion that the program should be abolished, regardless of whether it is replaced by another humanities program (several good and well-tried ones are available) or by an extended-basics program.

If the criticisms I shall address were nit-picking comments by a philosopher of education about an alternative philosophy with which he happens not to agree, this would not be enough to create doubt about the pedagogical benefits of this humanities curriculum. We would have to get into the classrooms and look for redeeming features. But in this case the errors are so gross that it is quite obvious that many, possibly most, students will be or have been seriously confused by teachers whose intellectual level (on these topics) is clearly unacceptable. Not only is there no hope of achieving the purposes of this curriculum, it is extremely likely that we are undermining students' native capacity to think sensibly about these issues.

---

[1] The author's references to program rationales, philosophy, overview, and so on all refer to material contained in Appendix B.

I do not claim that nothing valuable is being acquired from any of the lessons. The alternative to this humanities curriculum is not a sensory deprivation tank. The curriculum is indefensible unless its effects are *enormously better* than the same amount of time spent on assigned reading. That's the zero comparison level, because that involves (roughly) a saving of four salaried professional positions. To justify this curriculum, we have to show a probability of doing better than free reading/viewing of humanities materials already in or cheaply available to the school resource center. It's completely irrelevant to assert that some students pick up some useful and/or interesting stuff from this colossal investment of their precious time and the taxpayers' precious resources. Of course they will. The problems are:

(a) They may pick up a great deal that is confusing, or boring, or erroneous.

(b) They can pick up plenty of good ideas and experiences without any of the expenditure for this program.

(c) If something like the cost of this program is to be expended, a first-rate program can be provided, in the humanities or in other areas.

Let's get down to cases. This isn't a humanities program; it's an art appreciation program with a few footnotes on stray topics such as aging and the history of technology. Worse, it spends little time on the art forms that most people actually enjoy, thereby cutting back still further its chances of doing something worthwhile. It would be a waste of everyone's time to go into great detail about this. I will take up a few points, but many more could be made.

Whatever the justification may be for "art appreciation" or "aesthetic education," it has almost nothing to do with the justifications provided in the department's "Overview." The overview provides the usual plausible justifications for including in the curriculum some study of the meaning of life and the nature of humanity, that is, philosophy, psychology, moral education, anthropology. Even the list of "Specific Objectives"—which are only sporadically connected to the overview they are supposed to instantiate—lists critical thinking, multicultural understanding and cross-disciplinary connections as major objectives, none of which are even well exemplified in the arts areas, let alone well covered by considering only or mainly that area. Because these preliminary materials are mostly irrelevant rhetoric, the validity of the authorization process is seriously compromised, a further reason for suspension.

The justification for the curriculum as it actually emerges in the lesson topics, that is, the justification for aesthetic education *of this type and on this scale,* is nonexistent. A case can be made for some kind of aesthetic education as enrichment of the quality of leisure, perhaps as broadening the perspective of the citizen, but that justification isn't going to carry the burden of three years of compulsory study of elitist arts, a curriculum chunk that displaces a dozen curriculum components with much higher priority. That higher priority is not something I arbitrarily assert from outside. It is the priority or priorities referred to in the overview and general remarks and indeed the title of this program, a priority simply disregarded in the curriculum content.

How can one be sure these higher priorities are really disregarded in the actual lessons, without investigating them? Well, if they aren't, if the lessons *aren't* on the topics they are said to be on, the curriculum is not the one authorized, it was misrepresented, and it must be cancelled. If it *is* about those topics, the above criticisms, which are expanded below, are fatal.

Why couldn't some of these topics be treated in such a way as to bear fruit for the student in the dimensions of philosophy, psychology, critical thinking, and comparative anthropology? There are two parts to the answer. First, it's not enough that they have *some value;* the key question is whether they have *enough value* to compete with a direct approach. Second, everything we know about the transfer of learning makes it absolutely certain that the answer to the key question is negative. If you want to teach critical thinking, for example, you have to teach it with examples from a wide range of controversial areas, the very areas where you want the pay-off, not the most suspect of all areas for its application (art criticism is hardly a model of objective criticism). You must also teach it by using *materials aimed at teaching it,* with some methods outlined and some traps described; and, most important of all—use people who can do it right. (This faculty flunked the rather elementary critical thinking exercise of matching goals, rationale, and objectives.) If, to take another example, you want to teach surveys of knowledge in the "humanities, the social sciences, and the natural sciences," you have to do it directly and do it competently, or let them read about it and save yourself $100,000 a year. And so on. In short:

(a) There are excellent reasons for a curriculum that addresses the general issues about the nature of humanity which this curriculum is supposed to address.

(b) There are no reasons from the lesson topic list to think that this curriculum addresses them.

(c) If it does so, covertly, it runs into the "misleading advertising" charge.

(d) Misleadingly advertised or not, if it does so it is such an ineffective, indirect and incompetent approach to these matters that there can be no possible justification for continuing it.

(e) What *is* covered cannot possibly pay the freight for that large a slice of curriculum, and probably not for 20 percent of that slice (a judgment based on the values of the committee).

Some Footnotes

To the extent that the curriculum was converted into a vehicle for teaching writing and oral skills, it has at least that redeeming feature; but so would any substitute for it that had content more relevant to the major curriculum needs listed in the overview.

A good slice of the content actually turns out to be *philosophy* of art ("what is art," "what is style," and so on). The few substantial items provided make it clear that, apart from its really marginal justification, the performance here is also completely incompetent. Sample illustrations:

• The overview opens with a quote from philosopher Whitehead: "After you understand all about the sun and the stars and the rotation of the earth, you may still miss the radiance of the sunset." Good thought, but the program only talks about art, and their definition of a work of art explicitly excludes all natural phenomena such as sunsets. The quote is thus irrelevant to what it is supposed to illustrate. (Indeed, it reminds us that a needs or interest-driven aesthetic education program *should*— unlike this one—spend time on natural beauty, as well as the crafts, design, comics, graphics, and television, which are so conspicuously absent here.)

• Their definition of a work of art is so sloppy that it includes the organizational structure of the Pentagon, the arrangement of the endgame pieces on a chessboard, dropping the Hiroshima bomb, and the patch on a punctured inner tube as works of art. This is contrary to both the normal meaning of the term and the types of artwork included in the curriculum lessons. It's an unsound definition, but it seems even less sound to get the sixth grade into the philosophy of art.

Extraordinary confusions involving evaluation abound. For example, in response to a question from a board member about measuring impact on students, "the principal had said it can't be done statistically; the course did not teach children *what* to think and feel, it taught them *to* think and feel."

(a) One can perfectly well measure whether a course increases the amount of thinking and feeling without any evaluation of content.

(b) It's not true that the course does not teach them *what* to think; for example, it teaches them a definition of "work of art" (incorrect) and of many other terms, and it allegedly teaches them a hundred or a thousand historical facts, such as how Einstein's theories influenced the arts of the 20th century (one shudders to think what passed under that banner).

(c) A call to evaluate this course is made to us as if it had not already been evaluated. It *has* already been evaluated, at enormous expense, by a huge committee that met 30 times and which, I think, got about halfway to the right conclusion but had a failure of nerve or a rush of charity in the stretch. It should have used or been replaced by a couple of professionals working for a couple of days (on site in that case, since they would not have the data we have now); the results could scarcely have failed to be cheaper and better. *Which* professionals? Well, you can get a good look at options in this book. That they do not agree is irrelevant; a second committee wouldn't have agreed with the first.

In view of the above, the fact that the principal, assistant superintendent of curriculum, and the superintendent gave "strong personal endorsements" to this "humanities curriculum" raises some interesting further questions about personnel evaluation in Radnor township. (Perhaps that can be the subject of our next event in the Evaluation Triple Crown.)

In answer to your unspoken questions:

• *Isn't all this very mean?* No, it's either true or false. Truth-telling is the professional task of the evaluator, not being a friend or parent or PR representative.

• *Should anyone be this mean?* Yes; in this context.

• *Are you seriously suggesting that one can do armchair evaluation of a multi-year multi-instructor program?* Yes, occasionally.

• *Mightn't this be unfair to a dedicated faculty?* Dedicated is not enough; competence is also required, in the territory claimed. I have no reason to suppose the artist can't paint, or even teach painting. He or she sure can't define it, or teach critical thinking through it, though, and that's what he or she undertook to do.

• *Why take this tough a line?* Because evaluation is not psychotherapy. When evaluators get on-site, we start holding hands, we get co-opted into other roles. But this is one case where the seduction of the savior role can be avoided. And this is one case where the cost of a further evaluation can be avoided, if we speak honestly. Locally-designed curriculums, like locally-constructed tests, are about on a par with home-brewed medicine—once in a while you get lucky, but most of the time you get sick, and in this case, it is your children who suffer. They need strong medicine and a sound diet; this is soda pop and junk food. Something like 75 percent of them will graduate higher in their college class than the average teacher. It is not appropriate to assume that a teacher of such modest academic competence can construct a curriculum linking and illuminating the most elusive and abstract and important concepts that the best minds of several millenia have evolved. It will be hard enough for most teachers to teach these notions from good texts, let alone in their spare time write the texts—which is what they have in essence done here. And done in a thousand other schools—the lesson from this case is a general one, and a crucial one in U.S. education today.

5.
Using Professional Judgment

by Elliot W. Eisner

Elliot Eisner was a recent president of the National Art Education Association and is currently vice president of Division B—Curriculum Studies—of the American Educational Research Association. He questions the notion that evaluation must be highly technological and quantitative, calling instead for "educational connoisseurship" similar to criticism in the arts. Eisner is Professor of Education and Art, Stanford University, Stanford, California.

As I read the material describing the Radnor Middle School humanities program (Appendix B), I was struck by how carefully the committee had thought through its aims and goals, the concepts that were of central importance, the unique contributions of the various disciplines to the achievement of the program's aims, and to alternative approaches that could have been taken. Furthermore, the planning document itself is well written. It reflects a high level of sophistication in the arts and humanities, areas that are complex and often written about in obscure and perplexing ways. I mention these characteristics because they convey a high level of professional competency on the part of the planners and a willingness to consult and consider alternative courses of action in curriculum planning. The tone of the document reassures me that the group is not riding a bandwagon toward a destination neither they nor the drivers of the wagon understand. I am therefore—at the outset—quite favorably inclined toward the people who prepared this material.

I am also favorably inclined toward the aims they seek to achieve. It takes more than a little guts these days to attempt to develop a program in the humanities for adolescents. The push in most school districts is for a larger dose of the Three R's. Yet students should have access to important ideas about the nature of man; educational goals should include quality of experience as well as measureable competencies. American education would do well to have more such programs.

41

I mention these impressions and shared values partly because I don't want to give readers the illusion that evaluation, in order to be professional or competent, must be educationally neutral. Education is not a neutral enterprise. A neutral evaluator would not know how to begin or what to look for, having no bases for appraising educational merits. Without a value position, no evaluation could go forward.

I also want to let the reader know "where I'm coming from." I wish to make my own educational values clear and to avoid the seductive idea that somehow values do not exist for the evaluator. Having said this, let's turn to evaluation of the program. How might I go about this task if asked by the district to do so? There are a number of questions and issues I would try to address.

Curriculum Concerns

First, what is the purpose of the evaluation?[1] Are we interested in evaluating the educational merits of what is taught? Do we want to evaluate the quality of the teaching taking place in the program? Is our purpose to provide feedback to teachers about how things are going in their classrooms? Do we want to know what the outcomes of curriculum and instruction are? Each of these questions provides a very different focus for evaluation and each requires that a different content be attended to. For example, if we wanted to know about the quality of the curriculum, we would need to examine the content that was being taught. What are the central ideas constituting the curriculum? What concepts are focused upon? What general theoretical structures are being offered to the students on which these concepts can be placed?

Furthermore, we would want to know something about the kind of curriculum tasks children were asked to engage in. We can distinguish between content as such and the way in which it is embodied in curricular activities. How do students gain access to the ideas that are believed to be so important: by debate, through lecture, by viewing and discussing films, by reading? Thus, we would want to know about the curriculum as it has been planned in both the dimensions I have identified. But knowing there is often a slip between the cup and the lip, we would want to know how the plans were actually implemented in the classroom. Are teachers actually using the curriculum materials in a way consistent with the program's aims? What are the teachers doing that is in fact better than what

---

[1] For a discussion of the various functions evaluation can perform, see Elliot W. Eisner, *The Educational Imagination: On The Design and Evaluation of Educational Programs* (New York: The Macmillan Company, 1979).

was planned, and what things are not being done as well as was hoped for?

For these kinds of data classroom observation would be crucial. We would not only make some appraisal of the curriculum with respect to the quality of the ideas, concepts, and structures it makes available to students, but also with respect to the activities it employs to engage students so that these ideas are acquired and meaningful. Furthermore, we would want to determine the relationship between what was planned and what was implemented.

Perhaps the school board was really interested in what students were learning as a consequence of this course. To deal with that question, the focus of our attention would shift from the curriculum materials primarily to the process of classroom life and to what students are doing in those classrooms. When we ask what students are learning, we ask a question much broader than whether students are achieving course objectives.[2] If we use the latter frame of reference, we constrain our focus to the forms of learning that are intended. But it doesn't take an educational genius to recognize that students learn both a lot more and a lot less than what is intended. Furthermore, much of what they learn in a class cannot be predicted and much might not be educationally meritorious. Children can learn to dislike what they study as well as to like it.[3] If we want to assess the side effects of educational practice, the evaluation net we cast must be wider than what instructional objectives prescribe.

Student Outcomes

How do we get such data? How can we find out what children have learned? In the evaluation of this humanities program, there are several sources of data I would seek. First, I would spend a fair amount of time in the classroom preparing educational criticisms of what I had seen.[4] I would focus on the level of discourse the children were using, the extent

---

[2] It is useful to distinguish between objective oriented evaluation and outcome oriented evaluation. The former seeks primarily to determine whether or not the intended aims have in fact been achieved. The latter is concerned not only with these, but with other effects of the processes of teaching. Hence, the latter is far broader in scope than the former.

[3] Sensitivity to the ancillary consequences of teaching has been recognized by a variety of astute educators throughout the 20th century. John Dewey observed, "Perhaps the greatest of all pedagogical fallacies is the notion that a person learns only the particular thing he is studying at the time." In more current educational jargon, these effects are related to what has been referred to as the "hidden curriculum."

[4] For a discussion of educational connoisseurship and educational criticism, see Elliot W. Eisner, *The Educational Imagination.*

to which their comments were relevant and insightful regarding the material they were studying. I would examine the products they had produced: their essays, their drawings and paintings, the plays they had performed, and so forth. If possible, I would compare these with products they had produced earlier in the program.

If the program were having positive effects, I would expect to find a good deal of animation and richness in the discussions; I would expect to find depth of analysis and insight in students' comments and writings. I would hope the quality of their graphic work and performance was high. How would I judge such performance? Two ways. First, by comparing "pre" and "post" performance. Second, by comparing the students' work with that of other students I have encountered of the same SES. I would use my experience in education as the basis for appraising the work and discussions I observed.

I would also interview samples of students to find out what they thought they had gotten out of the course. In my interviews I would ask questions to determine the extent to which they were able to make connections between what they were taught in the course and issues pertaining to problems outside the school. I would seek evidence of transfer and the ability to recognize the connection between the several arts and humanities disciplines they were using in their studies. Finally, I might use some short-answer tests, but these would indeed be brief and designed simply to tap into the students' grasp of some of the concepts they were taught. I would be far more interested in the satisfaction and excitement they experienced in the course and the extent to which the course generated activities outside the school that had roots in the classroom.

When it comes to evaluation of student outcomes in programs that might be regarded as "open-ended" in character—humanities programs, arts programs, courses in creative writing, those courses not aiming at achievement of uniform outcomes—it is particularly important to assess the diversity of what students have learned in class. In the teaching of spelling and even in middle school and high school math courses, the answers to be achieved by students to common problems are themselves to be common across students. Uniformity of outcome when the answers are correct is the mark of effective teaching. In open-ended programs, diversity of outcome—when that diversity is educationally valuable—is a virtue: one seeks uniqueness and fresh interpretation in a student's treatment of an idea or product, not simply the ability to apply known operations to known problems in order to arrive at known ends.

Furthermore, effective humanities programs would be as much interested in the kinds of questions students were able to raise about what they have studied as they were about the kinds of answers they had. Is the program raising in the minds of students the kinds of questions that will feed them intellectually through life? A noble ambition for a middle school humanities course? Indeed it is. But worth seeking.

The Radnor humanities program makes explicit use of different disciplines for illuminating aspects of human nature. For example, it uses visual art and music as well as literature to tell students about the life of a culture.[5] I would want to know the extent to which students were becoming aware of the ways in which different forms of representation such as art, music, and literature, as distinct art forms, contributed to their understanding. Do the students recognize the unique contributions that different forms make to what they have come to know? This is, in a sense, an effort to assess the epistemology of the program. Can the students raise above the course content and appreciate the contents' more general functions? Such data could be secured by randomly sampling students and conducting structured interviews with them about what they had learned, and what each discipline told them about a particular topic.

Finally, with respect to the assessment of student outcomes, I would provide students with opportunities to convey what they had learned by asking them to select the particular *form of representation*[6] they felt most comfortable in using to display it. For some students, the essay would be the most appropriate vehicle. For others it might be painting, drama, or sculpture. For others the form used might be a play, a dance, or a photography exhibition. The point is to broaden the range of vehicles students can use to portray the concepts and theories, ideas and emotions they experienced in the course. Words will do quite well for some, but not all. I would want to make alternative forms of representation available to those students whose interests and aptitudes were in nonverbal forms of expression.

Classroom Processes

If the school board were interested in the quality of teaching, my focus in evaluation would again be on classroom processes, but with a special eye on the teachers. How do the teachers relate to the students? What kind of interest or enthusiasm do they generate? What is the nature of the questions they ask? To what extent do teachers model the skills

---

[5] The relationship between the form used to convey what one has come to know and the content being conveyed is discussed in Eisner, *Cognition and Curriculum: A Basis for Deciding What to Teach* (New York: Longman, Incorporated, in press).
[6] *Ibid.*

and attitudes the course wants students to acquire? What do teachers do in their teaching that is unique and valuable? What aspects of their teaching can be improved? Such questions, in addition to others that might emerge in the course of observation, would provide the data needed for evaluating the quality of teaching in the classroom. I probably would not use so-called objective observation schedules that are to be "ticked off" in various categories. What makes for excellence in teaching cannot be determined, I believe, by counting ticks on a grid. Teaching is much more subtle an affair. In addition, it is very difficult, indeed impossible, to reconstruct a vivid image of classroom teaching by examining such reductionist attempts at reporting: such data are simply too cryptic.

To avoid the kind of "objective reductionism" so typical of structured observation schedules, I would use the approach to evaluation that my students and I have developed at Stanford University called *educational connoisseurship and educational criticism*.[7] This approach requires that classrooms be observed intensively to secure the kind of information that competent attention to classroom processes makes possible. Those processes, when described, interpreted, and appraised in written narrative, have a family resemblance to the kind of writing that film, drama, and art critics create. The descriptive aspect of written educational criticism helps readers visualize what has transpired in classrooms. The descriptive language is rich, makes use of metaphor, attempts to render the spirit of the place. The interpretative aspect of educational criticism attempts to account for what has happened. It employs theory and concepts from the social sciences to explicate what has been described. It is intended to answer *why* what occurs has occurred, while the descriptive aspect attempts to provide a vivid account of the events themselves. Finally, the evaluative aspect of criticism renders some judgment of the educational value of what has been described and interpreted. It appraises the conditions and practices observed, described, and interpreted. The end in view is to help an audience grasp the educational meaning of what has taken place—in this case, the character and quality of teaching.

If the school board wanted this information for its confidential use—assuming I had permission from the teachers involved—I would write the report one way. If the report were to be read by teachers *and* the board, it would be written differently. If it were to be used only by teachers, it would be written still a third way. This chameleon-like approach to reporting rests on a simple premise: the aim of evaluation is to be helpful. To be helpful, an evaluation must address the audience for whom it is prepared. The same message is not necessarily suitable for everyone.

---

[7] See *The Educational Imagination.*

Overview

In my description of the evaluation of the Radnor School humanities program, three objects of attention have emerged. First, the curriculum itself is a potential subject for evaluation. Is the curriculum itself worth teaching? Are the concepts, generalizations, and theoretical structures educationally significant? Are the activities that carry them to students likely to be interesting and effective? Are the students likely to learn from them?

Second, the quality of teaching is an important dimension for appraisal. The focus would be on the teacher's relationship to students. It would appraise the ways in which the teacher mediated the curriculum, raised questions, led discussions, and modeled behavior consistent with program goals.

Third, the students and their work are important subjects for evaluation. We asked not only whether objectives were being attained, but what students were learning in the program. We were interested in unintended outcomes as well as those that were intended. And we were interested not only in the answers students had, but in the kinds of questions they could raise about important issues in the humanities.

These three foci—the curriculum, the character and quality of teaching, and the outcomes for students—are important points of focus for virtually any adequate educational evaluation. Nevertheless, the specific focus for the evaluation of this particular program would be developed through discussions with those in the school district seeking evaluation. The task of the evaluator in this phase is to help clients recognize the various uses to which evaluation practices can be put and to help them understand that different uses require different data. The first question addresses itself to the intended function of the evaluation. Once this question has been partially resolved (it is never totally resolved), the next steps for program evaluation can be taken.

6.
CIPP in Local Evaluation

by William J. Webster

Our only author employed as a full-time evaluator for a school district, William J. Webster has had a great deal of experience in implementing large-scale evaluation systems. Webster is Associate Superintendent for Accountability, Accreditation, and Information Systems, Dallas Independent School District, Dallas, Texas.

My evaluation of the humanities program relies heavily on the comprehensive CIPP (Context, Input, Process, Product) model developed by Stufflebeam and others.[1] CIPP defines evaluation as the process of delineating, obtaining, and providing useful information for judging decision alternatives. It identifies four major types of evaluation: context evaluation to feed planning decisions, input evaluation to feed programming decisions, process evaluation to feed implementing decisions, and product evaluation to feed recycling decisions.

Briefly, *context evaluation* provides a rationale for determining educational objectives by defining the pertinent environment, describing desired and actual conditions of the environment, identifying needs, and diagnosing problems that prevent needs from being met. *Input evaluation* assesses the capabilities of responsible agencies, identifies strategies for achieving the objectives determined through context evaluation, and suggests designs for implementing those strategies. Once a strategy has been selected, *process evaluation* provides feedback to the implementers of the plans and procedures to help them detect faults in the design or implementation and make necessary corrections. Finally, *product evaluation* provides assessment of the effects of educational programs; that is, it assesses the effects of the strategy selected through input evaluation to meet the need identified

---

[1] D. L. Stufflebeam and others, *Educational Evaluation and Decision-Making* (Itaska, Ill.: E. E. Peacock Publishers, 1971).

48

by context evaluation. Such assessment is completed in light of process evaluation data.

Figure 1 on page 50 presents a schematic of the CIPP model. The schematic may cover a period of one day or ten years, depending on the scope of the strategies to be evaluated. The reader may find it helpful to refer to Figure 1 throughout this chapter.

Context Evaluation

A prerequisite to improvement in any area is a knowledge of needs and performance levels. A context evaluation of sorts was conducted when the committee, considering the objectives of the program, voted unanimously that it should continue to exist, although the need was defined with few objective data. Ideally, the need for such a program would be determined on the basis of input from the community, teachers, administrators, parents, and students, relative to the services they wish their school system to provide. From the discrepancy between clients' desired services and those actually provided by the school district, a legitimate need for services is established.

Once the need has been defined, preliminary program planning begins. A small committee, similar to the Radnor Humanities Curriculum Review Committee, takes the needs assessment data collected during the context evaluation and attempts to design a program to meet those needs. In so doing, they use information on similar programs from other school systems to increase the probability of the program's success. Reviews of the literature, ERIC searches, and site visits to other school systems implementing similar programs are among the activities conducted during the input phase of the evaluation.

It would be useful to try to validate the objectives and strategies of the humanities program with its clients: the parents, students, and community.[2] In the validation process, the first step involves a meeting between the evaluator and the committee to clarify program goals and objectives. Then a survey instrument addressing specific objectives and organizational strategies is developed and sent to a random sample of community members, parents, students, and staff. This instrument determines whether or not the various clients of the school believe specific objectives of the program are valid. The objectives as well as the organizational structure are then refined, based on feedback from the survey and reviews of the literature in the humanities. If the results of the survey suggest the

---

[2] The first five diamonds and boxes in Figure 1 have been skipped and we pick up with the program implementation phase.

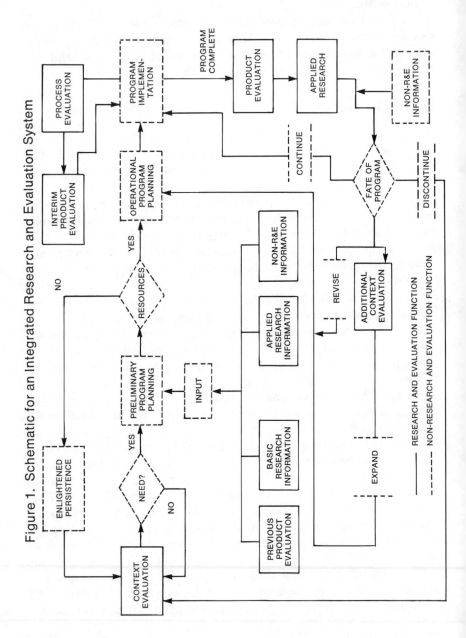

Figure 1. Schematic for an Integrated Research and Evaluation System

objectives are not valid in the eyes of the clients—a phenomenon often occurring in this day of tightening budgets and back-to-the-basics sentiment—then the program would probably have to go back to the drawing board for revisions and revitalization, or be scrapped.

Assuming the clients agree with the validity of the program objectives, the evaluator meets with the committee to generate a list of critical decisions to be made concerning the program, to determine the types of information necessary to make those decisions, and to plan the informational sources in such a way that critical decisions are precipitated by timely and objective information.

Instrumentation

The next step in planning the evaluation is design of the instrumentation. The course objectives and content suggest that three levels of instrumentation must be developed. The first involves instruments developed on the basis of content. These instruments are criterion-referenced tests designed to measure the concepts detailed in the specific course outlines (see Appendix B from p. 113). They are relatively straightforward and should be used largely in a formative sense to monitor student progress toward mastery of the specific content of the course units. If at all possible, it would be informative to use a comparison group of students who are not in the humanities program—but who are similar to Radnor students—to monitor programmatic effects on objective achievement. The instruments do not have to be strictly paper-and-pencil tests, but may involve manipulative exercises where appropriate.

The second level of instrumentation is development of classroom observation instruments to determine the extent to which the program has been implemened and to observe unintended outcomes. Public school programs are often not implemented as intended. Observation data, documenting that the program is operating as intended, protect the evaluator from evaluating imaginary events. This level of instrumentation obviously requires training classroom observers in the use of the observation instruments until they reach a determined level of interrater reliability.

The third level of instrumentation is by far the most difficult. At this level the evaluator attempts to determine the extent to which the program has met its overall objectives. It is entirely possible that a program such as Radnor's humanities curriculum could register positive effects on the first and second levels of instrumentation, but still fail to meet its overall objectives. Radnor's objectives included:

• Increasing students' aesthetic sensibilities; that is, the ability to respond affectively and cognitively to a variety of aesthetic experiences.

- Increasing students' proficiency in critical thinking skills (making and defending value judgments) and in creative thinking (selecting and synthesizing to solve problems).

- Helping students understand and appreciate human achievements in the arts: literature, drama, film, music, the visual arts, architecture, and dance.

- Increasing students' understanding and appreciation of their own social and cultural heritage while gaining greater understanding of and appreciation for the Judeo-Christian tradition and the African and Oriental cultures.

- Helping students understand the interrelatedness among seemingly disparate disciplines and increasing their ability to locate and describe patterns.

- Reinforcing students' oral and written communication skills.

Since the humanities curriculum represents a three-year course of study, this portion of the evaluation is conducted in phases. The concepts dealt with through the program are approached developmentally; that is, they are measured at the completion of specific years of the program. Regardless of the time frame used to approach each concept, it is obvious that strictly paper-and-pencil tests are inadequate for measuring most of the objectives. Rather, they should be measured in large part through observational techniques that record individual student responses to specific stimuli related to the objectives.

Evaluation Design

Once the instrumentation is designed and validated, the evaluator develops a detailed program evaluation design specifying the criteria by which the program is to be judged. This step involves continuous interaction between program personnel and the evaluator if the resulting information is to be maximally useful. While this close relationship is important, it is also essential that the evaluator retain independence from the program. Under no circumstances should the evaluator be assigned administratively to the program manager; such an arrangement would seriously undermine the objectivity of the evaluation.

Figure 2. Necessary Steps in Program Evaluation

1. Determine program objectives
   a. Meet with decision makers and program managers to determine program objectives.

    b. Refine objectives through thorough analysis, reviewing literature, questioning decision makers, analyzing input data, and so on.

2. Identify decisions and sources of information
   a. Using the objectives, meet with decision makers to generate a list of the critical decisions to be made concerning the objectives and the program.
   b. Determine the types of information necessary to make the various decisions.
   c. Estimate the critical decisions and plan the information sources so those decisions receive the most information.

3. Define measurable objectives and related decisions
   a. Work with project personnel to mold objectives so they may be measured.
   b. Operationalize the basis for decision making to relate to measured achievement of objectives.

4. Plan evaluation dissemination
   a. Identify the various audiences of the evaluation and estimate the level of sophistication of each intended audience.

5. Identify measuring instruments
   a. Review objectives and decisions and evaluate existing instruments to determine which can be used in the evaluation.
   b. Determine areas where no satisfactory instruments are available and develop complete specifications of instruments to be constructed.

6. Develop and test instruments.
   a. Develop needed instruments.
   b. Test new instruments, if necessary, on a sample of subjects.
   c. Refine new instruments on the basis of these tests.
   d. Test administration of any unconventional instruments or observation procedures.

7. Schedule information collection
   a. Specify sampling procedures to be used.
   b. Determine the schedule of observations and the instruments to be administered at each observation point.
   c. Schedule the personnel needed to administer instruments.

8. Organize data analysis
   a. Determine various formats of data including card and tape format specifications at various stages of collection and analysis. Specify processing necessary to put data into correct format at each stage of analysis.
   b. Plan nonstatistical analysis of data and resources necessary to perform analysis.

      c. Plan statistical analysis of data and programs necessary to analyze data.
      d. Determine which programs are already written and ready to use, which are written but need modifications to handle data in their intended formats, and which programs need to be written with specifications of these programs.

9. Design formal evaluation/research
    a. Prepare design including specifications of:
      • objectives
      • instrumentation
      • analysis methodology
      • data collection and reporting schedules
      • sampling procedures
      • data analysis schedules
      • final reporting schedules
    b. Type, print, and collate design.
    c. Disseminate formal design.

10. Develop computer program
    a. Develop necessary programs for analysis
    b. Modify existing programs
    c. Run all programs to be used on sample data in the proper medium and format. Construct sample data to simulate problems in actual data (mispunching, missing data, and so on).

11. Context evaluation
    a. Collect or supervise and coordinate collection of context evaluation information.
    b. Prepare context evaluation information for analysis.

13. Product evaluation
    a. Collect or supervise and coordinate the collection of product evaluation information.
    b. Prepare product evaluation information for analysis.

14. Analyze interim data
    a. Organize interim data.
    b. Perform analyses of interim data.

15. Report on formative evaluation
    a. Prepare formative evaluation reports.
    b. Type, print, and collate formative evaluation reports.
    c. Disseminate formative evaluation reports to project management and staff.

16. Analyze summative data
    a. Organize summative data.
    b. Perform analyses of summative data.

17. Report on summative evaluation/research
    a. Prepare the various summative evaluation/research reports for each audience; include objectives, findings, and recommendations expressed in an appropriate manner for each intended audience. This preparation includes the abstract of the report.
    b. Have report carefully proofread and corrected.
    c. Type, print, and collate the summative evaluation reports.
    d. Disseminate the summative evaluation/research reports to project personnel, district management, and the board of education.

18. Interpret reports
    a. Meet with project personnel to interpret reports.
    b. Meet with district management and the board of education to aid in report interpretation.

19. Disseminate reports further
    a. Disseminate summative evaluation/research reports to district administrators and interested professional staff.
    b. Prepare and disseminate a book of evaluation and research abstracts to professional staff.

20. Report feedback
    a. Meet with decision makers to obtain feedback regarding the report to improve reporting activities.

Reporting

The process depicted in the Figure 1 schematic has progressed to the program implementation stage. At this point, the evaluator's role becomes one of providing continuous formative evaluation reports about program implementation. These reports fall primarily into two categories, process evaluation and interim product evaluation. Process evaluation has three major objectives: (1) to detect defects in procedural design or its implementation, (2) to provide information for program decisions, and (3) to maintain a record of the implementation procedure as it occurs.

Interim product evaluation keeps program management informed about the attainment of specific subobjectives during the implementation phase. Thus, process and interim product evaluation reports inform program management about implementation and goal attainment levels while program adjustments are still possible.

The product evaluation phase could be approached in one of two ways. Since the humanities program is a three-year course, the most rational evaluation approach would be to design a three-year longitudinal study and trace current sixth-graders through the eighth grade. Taking that approach, the evaluator would collect data and provide them to program decision makers in interim evaluations through the early stages of the program, and then evaluate the overall objectives of the program after students who started it in the sixth grade had completed most of the eighth grade. To clarify the analysis, it would be helpful to use either a comparison group as a benchmark against which to judge program effects, or a multiple observation longitudinal design. In the best of all worlds, the evaluator would implement a multiple observation longitudinal design with a comparison group.

Realizing that most boards of education are not willing to wait three years for a product evaluation report, the realistic approach to product evaluation would involve design of a three-year study that would report certain aspects at the end of each school year.

The next phase of the evaluation is applied research. Through applied research, the evaluator determines combinations of learning styles, teaching styles, and program materials that optimize learning. The nature of this program precludes applied research studies. Such studies would be costly and probably could not be justified by the additional information gained from their outcomes.

Decision Making

Once the evaluator has completed the evaluation and provided the data to decision makers, a decision about the future of the program is made. However, there are many nonquantitative, and often very subjective, considerations that enter into decisions. The evaluation report is generally only one of many bases on which decisions are made. As shown in Figure 1, there are four primary choices.

First, decision makers can choose to continue the program in its current setting. If so, the summative product evaluation report becomes the context evaluation information for the next phase, and program implementation begins. This alternative usually occurs when decisions are made on the basis of longitudinal studies (where it is expected that results will not be evident after a relatively short implementation period). In the case of the humanities program, such a decision, coming after a three-year study, would call for no further evaluation.

A second alternative is to discontinue the program. This is usually done after product evaluation studies show that the program failed to meet its objectives or that it is simply not cost-effective. (Failure to meet objectives is often a necessary but insufficient reason to end a program.) Once a program is discontinued, the system returns to context evaluation, and once again applies the needs assessment and orientation phases.

If the product evaluation information is favorable, and it is practically and politically possible, the program may be expanded to serve additional students. Before making such a decision, additional context evaluation information must be examined to see if similar needs exist elsewhere. If such needs are demonstrated, then the program may be expanded to other settings and the program planning stage entered to extend the program. The extent of continued evaluation to be implemented under either the expansion or continuation alternatives is determined by decision makers with advice from the evaluation personnel.

A fourth alternative involves program revision, most of which should be accomplished on the basis of process and interim product evaluation reports. Often, however, summative product evaluation reports reveal weaknesses in portions of programs that would otherwise appear to be functional. In this instance, the summative product evaluation report becomes the context evaluation information for the next program planning cycle.

Evaluation is a continuous, essential part of any program implementation. Without valid and reliable evaluative data, it is very difficult for program managers and district decision makers to make intelligent, cost-effective decisions. Contrary to the belief expressed by many educators that evaluation is too costly, it is, rather, imperative to administrative decision making.

7.
Journal Entries of an Eclectic Evaluator

by Blaine R. Worthen

Blaine Worthen is known for the significant evaluations he has conducted, including the award-winning adversary evaluation of the Hawaii 3 on 2 program. He has organized and led several ASCD institutes on curriculum evaluation. A contributor to evaluation training methods, Worthen considers himself an eclectic evaluator and cautions others against unthinking adherence to the various models. In this chapter, he offers his pointers in a whimsical but earnest fictitious account. Worthen is Professor and Head, Department of Psychology, Utah State University, Logan.

At first, I was fooled by ASCD's request that led to this paper. The task appeared straightforward enough. "Would you," ASCD editor Ron Brandt had asked over the telephone, "be willing to write a chapter for a book on evaluation? We will give you a description of a real school program—sort of a case study—and would like you to explain, in a general way, how you would go about evaluating it." Straightforward. Simplicity itself, right?

Wrong. Through daily association with more clinically oriented colleagues in a psychology department, I have gained considerable insight lately into the subtleties of human behavior and discourse. I have learned, for example, when a student wishes me a "Merry Christmas," to look beyond this socially acceptable salutation to ponder deeper levels of probable motivation and meaning. Similarly, when a colleague brands my pet idea as "singularly stupid," I pause to wonder what he really meant by that. Such heightened awareness should have led me to probe the ASCD request more carefully, to look beyond the obvious. But the task seemed inherently interesting; the chance to be associated in the same volume with distinguished colleagues like Scriven, Stake, Popham, Brickell, and so on was tempting; and Ron Brandt seemed like such a decent chap. So I agreed.

Then the "case study" arrived from ASCD, a description of a humanities curriculum in a middle school in the Radnor Township (Pennsylvania)

58

School District. It contained the report of the Humanities Curriculum Review Committee which appears as Appendix B in this publication, and the brief overview that now appears as the introduction. I read the material quickly, worried vaguely that the description was so incomplete that it might not provide much focus for an evaluation, and then dropped the missive into my ASCD file, since the deadline was still months away.

Months passed. So did the deadline. A skillfully worded reminder from the editor prodded my conscience, and I retackled the task, beginning by re–reading the program description sent by ASCD. I had been right. The writing was lucid, it provided a general outline of the humanities program, gave the general context and some issues surrounding it, and even provided some details about rationale, objectives, schedules, and the like. But it struck me as not nearly enough. Somehow, I have never learned to design an evaluation that is really "on-target" without knowing a good bit about not only the program but also the educational and political context in which it is embedded, the personnel who operate it, the population it is intended to serve, availability of resources for the program (not to mention the evaluation), and so on. Without such information, deciding how to aim the evaluation is largely guesswork, and the odds are high that it will miss the mark. How, I wondered, could ASCD expect any evaluator to make a clean hit on such a fuzzy target?

To put it bluntly, I felt caught, frustrated at the realization that it simply was not feasible to get a clear enough picture of the program and the factors influencing it to permit me to design an evaluation I would feel comfortable defending. Were I like some of my more clairvoyant colleagues who seem not to need much information about a program to launch a full-fledged evaluation, or like the enviably certain and single-minded souls I know who push and pull every evaluation problem until it can be solved by their preferred evaluation approach, I might have worried less. But somehow I have been afflicted with an abiding conviction that the evaluation approach should be tailored to fit the evaluation problem or need, not the reverse. So I continued to fret about the ambiguity of the request.

Then suddenly the realization hit me. The fuzziness of that target was no accident—it was really a cleverly contrived narrative inkblot, a thinly disguised analog to the Rorschach. By providing purposefully incomplete information about the Radnor humanities curriculum, each author would be forced to complete the picture with pigments from his own evaluation psyche, to fill in the gaps, the missing pieces, and in so doing, to reveal clearly the personal preferences and predilections that make each evaluator's approach unique and render evaluation still more of an art than a science.

Having thus applied my newly acquired clinical insight to discover the real intent hidden within ASCD's outlined task, I can now approach it without the unease that troubled me earlier. Opportunities for public self-analysis come but rarely to the evaluator. So, join me on an introspective excursion. And meanwhile, should an ASCD editor ever wish you "Seasons Greetings," . . .

My Evaluation "Model"

One facet of my assignment was stated thus: "Because we are interested in illustrating a variety of approaches, we would appreciate your using your 'model' of evaluation to the extent that you can."

Such a request may not seem unreasonable, but it puzzled me somewhat, for two reasons. First, I have never written or promulgated anything that purported to be an evaluation model. Indeed, I have argued that none of the writings in the field of evaluation really qualify as "models" in any meaningful sense of the word (although they are very useful in other ways), and that unthinking discipleship to the so-called models is among the most serious impediments to improving the practice of evaluation.[1]

Second, I am a self-confessed eclectic in my own evaluation work, designing each evaluation *de novo*, using pieces of the so-called "models" only if they seem relevant and appropriate. Certain features of some models I use frequently, others seldom or never. While I have developed some preferences of my own in doing evaluations, the great majority of what I do is application of what I have distilled from others' ideas. But much as I am influenced by the impact of my colleagues' thinking, I can recall only one or two instances in the past decade where I have conducted an evaluation in adherence to any "model" of evaluation. Rather, I find greater relevance in tailoring by "snipping and sewing" together bits and pieces off the more traditional ready-mades and even weaving a bit of homespun, if necessary, to cover the client's needs. In short, I seem a poor candidate to discuss how I would apply my "model" of evaluation.

If I have grown to care for and use any one evaluation approach more than others, it would be what I have termed the "multiple method" approach to evaluation. Based loosely on the logic of measurement "triangulation," it is a flexible approach that can be readily adapted to allow use and combination of multiple frames of reference, multiple sources of information, multiple data collection strategies and techniques, and so on. It

---

[1] A rationale for these assertions is contained in B. R. Worthen, "Eclecticism and Evaluation Models: Snapshots of an Elephant's Anatomy?" Presented at the annual meeting of the American Educational Research Association, New York, April 1977.

proposes collection of information from diverse sources, using diverse instruments derived from diverse points of view. Intended to reduce bias and error resulting from a more narrow focus, such an approach recognizes plurality of values and information needs. Although neither my unique conception nor my "model" of evaluation, this approach would be more characteristic of my evaluation work than any other I could imagine. So, I asked the editor if this was what he had in mind as my evaluation model.

Well, not really. I was supposed to illustrate the so-called "adversary model." If that model belongs to anyone, however, it is Egon Guba, who first suggested it, or to Tom Owens, who first used it and wrote about it, or perhaps to Bob Wolfe, who codified parts of it and has championed its use broadly. I have merely used it (and possibly abused it), critiqued it, and tried to write analytically about strengths and weaknesses I see as inherent in any adversarial approach to evaluation.[2] Aside from that, I have little taste for adversarial behavior, especially if my adversary is bigger, faster, or brighter than me (and almost everyone I know fits in at least one of those categories).

But I did promise to try to work the adversary model in if and where I felt it were appropriate (being eclectic, of course).

An Evaluator's Journal and Archival Traces

In keeping with my view that this evaluation is primarily a projective exercise, I have taken the liberty of imagining that the evaluation has already been planned, thus permitting description of what has already happened in the design stage. This shift in tense is important, since it allows exploration of the interactive, iterative nature of evaluation design, which is difficult to see when one looks only at the artificially one-dimensional evaluation plan.

I have chosen to use imaginary journal entries and file artifacts to communicate many of my thoughts about how the evaluation might be conducted. In doing so, I have liberally interpreted the Radnor context; I have made many assumptions about what went on as the evaluation unfolded; I have invented fictional characters[3] and events to suit my purposes; and in the process I have probably unintentionally maligned at least some of the principal actors in the Radnor drama. Hopefully, I have at

---

[2] For example, see B. R. Worthen and W. T. Rogers, "The Pitfalls and Potential of Adversary Evaluation," *Educational Leadership* 37 (April 1980): 536-543; and B. R. Worthen and T. R. Owens, "Adversary Evaluation and the School Psychologist," *Journal of School Psychology* (Winter 1978): 334-345.

[3] Any resemblance to persons living or dead is purely coincidental.

least done so equitably. My sincere apologies are extended to Principal Janson and others for any violence I may have done to their school system or sensibilities.

My journal entries cover a six-week period during the design of the evaluation plan for the humanities program. I have also annotated these entries and artifacts under "author comments" to help underscore important points.

Planning the Evaluation

November 2, 1979. *Received an interesting call today from a Mrs. Janson, principal of a middle school in Radnor Township (somewhere near Philadelphia). She asked if I might be willing to undertake an evaluation of a somewhat controversial humanities curriculum in her school. Seems board of education members have asked for the evaluation. I agreed tentatively (having just received the cost estimate for Brad's orthodontics), but told her I couldn't make a final commitment without knowing more about the program, precisely why they want it evaluated, what use they would make of the evaluation findings, the resources available for the evaluation study, and so on. She promised to send some written materials for me to review.*

Author comments. To agree to undertake an evaluation without first knowing a good bit about the program to be evaluated strikes me as a potential disservice to both the program and the evaluator. Only an evaluator who is naive, avaricious, or supremely confident that his or her evaluation skills or approach will solve any evaluation problem would plunge in with so little information. Having once met all three of those criteria, I have more recently repented, and during the last decade have insisted on learning enough about the program, prior to committing to evaluate it, to be certain I could be of some help.

*　　*　　*

November 8. *Spent a few minutes this evening reading through materials I received from Radnor Township School District. They sent a brief report of their Humanities Curriculum Review Committee, which listed committee membership; outlined their activities; gave goals, objectives, and rationale for the curriculum; and included an outline of the proposed content and a schedule for implementation. They also listed other alternatives they had considered and rejected, even explaining why, which is a helpful inclusion. No clue in the materials, however, to some of* *the more important things I need to know before I decide whether I can be of any real help to them. Spent a while jotting down some questions I want to ask the principal.*

Author comments. Later examination of artifacts in my "Radnor School District Evaluation" file would reveal the following list of questions.

Artifact No. 1

1. How old is the humanities curriculum in the Radnor School District? The humanities curriculum review committee was launched in 1978, just over a year ago—but what about the curriculum? Is it well-established or new? Entrenched or struggling to find root?

2. Have there been any previous efforts to evaluate the humanities program? If so, by whom, when, what were the findings, and how did they affect the program?

3. Why does the board want the program evaluated now? What are the political forces at work? If it is controversial, who are the advocates (beyond the obvious)? The opponents? What sparks the controversy?

4. What decision(s) will be made as a result of the evaluation? Will the evaluation really make a difference, or is it merely for show?

5. How broadly did the curriculum committee sample opinions of the public, the students, teachers, administrators, outside specialists? To what extent did those groups really have a chance to give input? Were they well enough informed for their input to be on target? How much do they feel they were really listened to—did their input really shape the outcome?

6. How well is the humanities department at Radnor School integrated with the other departments? Is the relationship congenial, competitive? Any problems here?

7. What are the costs of the humanities program (dollars, time)? Any problems here?

8. What resources are available to conduct the evaluation? How good a job do they really want? (If evaluation budget is inadequate, are there staff members in the school or district who might be assigned to spend time helping collect some of the data, working under my supervision? May not cost much less overall, considering staff time, but should substantially reduce cash outlay for the district, for consultant time, travel, per diem. Use this only in areas where bias isn't too much of a concern or where I can check and correct pretty well for any bias that creeps in.)

9. What access will I have to collect the data I need? Are there any problems with the teachers' association or contracts, policies on testing

students, and so forth, that would constrain me if I wanted to observe classrooms, interview teachers or test students? What about policies concerning control of the evaluation report(s), review or editorial rights they may insist on, my rights to quote, release, and so on?

10. Are there any other materials that might give me a better feel for the program? What about the unit lesson plans the schedule says should be developed by now?

11. And lest I forget. Rhetoric aside, are they really serious about attaining *all* the goals they have laid out? In a mere two hours per week over three school years? Or are those goals just windowdressing to sell the program?

Author comments. Most of these questions simply seek descriptive information essential to know how (or whether) to conduct the evaluation. Questions 3, 4, 5, 7, 8, and 11 may also suggest a hint of cynicism or suspicion; yet, the failure to ask and answer such questions has sent more rookie evaluators baying down wrong trails, en route to unproductive thickets of irrelevant findings, than any other single oversight.

*   *   *

November 9. *Called Mrs. Janson, principal of Radnor Middle School. She responded to several of my questions, but as we got into the discussion, it became apparent that she couldn't really answer some of them without presuming to second-guess the board or others. After a bit, she asked, in view of all the questions I was posing, how much information I really thought I would need before I could sit down and outline an evaluation design that would tell them what they needed to know. I pointed out that was precisely the problem. I wasn't yet certain just what it was they needed to know; hence all my questions. I suggested to Mrs. Janson that the most feasible way to proceed would be for me to visit the school for two or three days, talk with her and some other members of the committee (including a parent or two), visit with some board members, observe some humanities classes, review the written units, and see if I couldn't get my questions answered, along with a lot of other questions that will probably occur to me in the process. I suggested that I could then leave with her a rough draft of an evaluation plan that I thought would answer their questions; they could review it and decide if they wanted me to proceed with any or all of it. That way they would know in advance how I intended to carry out the evaluation and what data I proposed to collect, rather than discovering at the end of the evaluation that they didn't really place much stock in the approach I had used or that I had omitted infor-*

mation they viewed as critical. Mrs. Janson immediately saw the wisdom and advantage in my suggestions. She seems delightfully perceptive. Arranged to visit Radnor next week.

Author comments. In reaching agreements about the conduct of an evaluation, the evaluator should not be the only person to exhibit caution. Those responsible for the program being evaluated (referred to hereafter as "clients" for the sake of convenience) should also look carefully at what is proposed before they commit precious resources to the evaluation. While most evaluators of my acquaintance are well-intentioned, and a majority of those competent, there are yet too many charlatans and hucksters who lack the scruples and/or the skills necessary to do good evaluation work. Atrocities committed by such have gone far to breed skepticism that many educators extend undeservedly to well-qualified, reputable evaluators. Even with well-intentioned, competent evaluators, potential clients can have no assurance *a priori* that their particular approach to evaluating the program will be very helpful.

It is for these reasons that I generally suggest that the evaluator and client interact enough to clarify in some detail what the evaluator is proposing before they "plight their troth." This might require the client to invest a small amount of resources to cover out-of-pocket expenses and a day or two's time for the evaluator (or more than one evaluator) to talk with representatives of the various audiences for the evaluation, probe areas of unclarity, and provide at least a rough plan to which the client can react. In my judgment, that type of small investment will yield important returns to the client and avoid the later disenchantment that often occurs as an evaluation unfolds in ways never imagined by a client (but perhaps envisioned all along by the evaluator).

The best possible results of such a "preliminary design" stage are sharper, more relevant focusing of the evaluation and clarity of understanding that will undergird a productive working relationship between evaluator and client throughout the study. The worst that can happen is that a small proportion of the resources will be spent to learn that there is a mismatch between what the evaluator can (or is willing to) deliver and what the client needs. That is small cost compared to the alternative of discovering the mismatch only after the evaluation is well underway, the resources largely expended, and an untidy divorce the only way out of an unsatisfactory relationship.

*   *   *

November 14. *Just completed an interesting day and evening in the Radnor School District trying to get a fix on their humanities* *program. Had informative discussions with Mrs. Janson, Mr. Holton (chairman of the committee), two humanities teachers, and one parent who served on the committee. All are staunch "loyalists" for the program, but they don't seem close-minded about it. Not that they are really clamoring for an evaluation—I gather that interest comes mostly from the board— but they seem open to looking at the program and have been candid in responses to my questions. The humanities teachers were the most guarded; not too surprising, I suppose, for it appears they may have a lot at stake. They and Mrs. Janson were all quick to record their skepticism about using tests and statistics to measure something as ethereal as the humanities. The humanities teachers seemed dumbfounded to learn that my Ph.D. is not in some branch of the humanities. One asked how anyone except an expert in humanities could presume to evaluate a humanities curriculum. I countered by pointing out that I write doggerel, publish an occasional short story, and once even tried to sell an oil painting. He wasn't easily impressed. I debated whether to trot out my well-practiced arguments about why evaluators need not be specialists in the content of what they evaluate, but decided the moment was not right for conversion.*

I asked each person I talked with what questions they would like an evaluation study to answer and how they would use the findings. I'll do the same tomorrow and then make up a master list.

Also read lesson plans for several of the units. No obvious cues there, except that some units appear to focus more on stuffing students with facts than engaging them in higher level mental processes that might better help them attain the lofty goals they've set for the curriculum. I'll need to look at some other lesson plans to see if I just pulled a biased sample. Also observed a humanities class in action, much of which focused on varying styles used by artists in the different art periods.

What have I learned so far? Quite a bit, I think, but I'll wait until I complete tomorrow before I try to summarize it.

Author comment. Although this journal entry may not really reflect a full day's work for the ambitious evaluator, it reflects some of the types of information the evaluator might try to obtain in informal interviews and perusal of written information and other materials. While the evaluator's thoughtfully prepared questions might be the core of such interviews, often the most useful information comes from probing leads that open during the conversation. Rogerian counseling may yet contribute useful skills to educational evaluation.

The discovery that the evaluator is not a specialist in the content or processes at the heart of the program being evaluated is often a rude shock to the client who is honestly confused as to how such a neophyte in the relevant subject matter could possibly be of help. Having reflected and written about this problem,[4] I used to try to convert clients with repeated and lengthy appeals to reason. Experience (and exhaustion) have convinced me of the wisdom of eschewing such appeals in favor of simple promises to obtain judgments of relevant substantive experts as part of the evaluation. Invoking patience is infinitely easier than persuasion and, in this case, seems as productive, since I have never had a client continue to worry this point after they have seen how relevant content expertise plays a part in the evaluation design.

*   *   *

November 15. *Met with three members of the board of education for lunch. Found them all frankly skeptical, in varying degrees, about the value of the middle school's humanities curriculum. One, an engineer, really seemed to have his mind made up. He described the humanities curriculum as a "puff course," and argued there was greater need for more formal reading instruction and work in the sciences at this age level and that the "interdisciplinary frills" could wait until students had mastered the basics. He forecast the outcome of "any honest evaluation" with such certainty that I suspect he may be impervious to any evaluative data that may show the program to have merit.*

The other board members seemed less definite, but both called for a rigorous, tough evaluation that will "tell it like it is." The board president indicated the program had never been formally evaluated and she felt it was difficult to defend continuation of a program, about which serious questions were being raised, in the absence of objective measurements that show it is working. We talked at length about program costs, what decisions will result from the evaluation, and who will make them. A most useful interview, especially when I got them to list the questions they would like to see addressed by the evaluation. I think the board is leaning, but have not yet made up their minds.

Spent the morning reviewing another set of lesson plans. No factsheets these; on the contrary, they contained much that strikes me as esoteric for the seventh-grader. But I'll await the judgment of humanities experts on that one.

Author comments. Before beginning any evaluation that relates to continuation or termination of a program, I always try to ferret out whether

---

[4] B. R. Worthen, "Content Specialization and Educational Evaluation: A Necessary Marriage?" Presented at the annual meeting of the American Educational Research Association, Chicago, April 1974.

there is really any need to evaluate—that is, have those who hold the power to make the decision already made up their minds (with little probability they will change them), regardless of the results of the study? That perspective stems from the sad realization that perhaps 75 percent of my first several years as an evaluator was spent generating methodologically impeccable but altogether useless evaluation reports—useless because I wasn't sharp enough to recognize the symptoms of ritualistic evaluation.[5]

Now this doesn't mean that one aborts every evaluation where the decision makers are found to be tilted toward one view or another. To take that stance would be to eliminate evaluations of most programs governed by human beings. But it does mean that one should check and be convinced there really are decision alternatives that the evaluation can influence. If not, I can muster little defense for the expenditure of time and money to carry out the study.

*   *   *

November 15 (continued). *This afternoon I met again with Mrs. Janson, then with a third humanities teacher, and finally with two teachers, one each from the English and social science departments. Now I feel a need to boil down all the rough notes I've taken to try to see what I have learned and what I yet need to learn about the program. That should help me be ready for the special session Mrs. Janson has arranged with the committee tomorrow.*

Artifact No. 2

Memo to the File

November 15, 1979

Re: Radnor Humanities Program: Summary of Information Learned On-site, November 14-15.

1. Radnor Township School District has had a humanities curriculum for 10 or 11 years, but it has evolved and mutated several times. With the exception of the additional structure and more skill emphasis, the current program has not changed greatly since about 1976.

2. The humanities curriculum has never been formally evaluated.

3. During the past year or two, community concerns have risen about the need for more academic content, more basic skills development, etc.,

---

[5] Evaluation where if the results come out right they will be used to support a preconceived position, but if they come out wrong they will be suppressed or ignored.

and the humanities curriculum has come to be viewed increasingly as a frill by important segments of the community, including some board members.

4. "Values clarification" does not appear to be a real issue, except in the minds of a strident few (including one committee member). The real issue seems to be that of devoting more time to the basic subjects vs. spending it on an interdisciplinary program aimed at using the arts to help students "understand and appreciate all that it means to be human." The differences appear to be honest ones of philosophy and conviction, not those of convenience or self-interest, at least for the most part. Although there is no public outcry evident, the skepticism reflected by the board seems to reflect the trend in the community (as perceived by those involved).

5. The curriculum committee made no systematic effort to obtain input from a broad or representative sampling of parents or others prior to their October report. They did hold public meetings attended by some parents, and parents on the committee reported conversations they had had with other parents, but community input was really quite limited.

6. The humanities department is isolated physically in a separate building from the other departments with which it might be expected to be integrated. There does not appear to be much integration across the departments.

7. The fiscal costs of the humanities program really reside in the collective salaries of the four humanities teachers (close to $80 thousand in total). There are no texts or other significant dollar costs. There does appear to be an interest on the part of some board members in the possible savings if the program were eliminated, since the board has expressed interest in making any staff reductions that might be made without reducing the quality of schooling offered to its students.

8. "Opportunity costs" are a key issue for those in the community who favor the "back-to-basics" notion discussed above. Within the school, faculty members in science and social science are particularly concerned about this, since time spent on their subjects was cut back to make room for the required humanities courses.

9. Within the school, faculty members in the science and social science departments are reported to be generally unenthusiastic about the program, those in the reading department about evenly split for and against it, and those in the English department generally favorable. The latter may relate to the fact that some of the humanities teachers apparently have good credentials in English, plus more seniority in the district than the current staff in the English department. If humanities folds, those staff members might be given jobs in the English department, putting jobs of some of the English faculty on the line. Support under those circumstances may be more pragmatic than idealistic.

10. The board really wants to make a "go-no go" decision and is asking for a summative evaluation to provide them with information to help them decide intelligently. All my instincts tell me that, if there were no evaluation, or if the evaluation were not credible to the board, they would ultimately discontinue the program. But I am equally convinced that an evaluation showing the program to be producing the benefits its sponsors claim for it could yield a positive board decision to allow its continuation.

11. There is apparently about $3,000 available for the evaluation this school year, with any subsequent follow-up funding (if necessary) to be decided by the board. The district is willing to assign some of its staff to assist in collecting data specified by the evaluator.

12. District policy will permit me access to whatever data sources I need. The district would not restrict my rights to quote, use, or release the report at my discretion.

13. There are no other written materials at present beyond the unit lesson plans I have reviewed. Other lesson plans are under development.

14. The staff does seem genuine about the program's goals, although some awareness seems to be creeping in that it may be difficult to help students understand "all that it means to be human" in a lifetime, let alone two hours a week for 27 months.

15. The primary audiences for the evaluation seem to be: (1) the board; (2) the humanities curriculum study committee; and (3) district and school staff not included on the committee but influenced by the outcomes. Important secondary audiences would include parents and students.

16. There is a sharp difference in the type of data preferred by the various audiences. Mrs. Janson represented the point of view of the humanities department staff and a majority of the committee when she said, "Numbers won't tell the story—this type of program defies quantitative evaluation." Board members called for hard data, however, with one saying, "If you can't quantify it somehow, it probably doesn't exist." Others noted they found testimonials unconvincing and would hope for something more substantial. When informed of those sentiments and asked to react to them in light of her own pessimism about quantitative measurement of student outcomes in humanities, Mrs. Janson said she would love to see some good "numerical" proof that the program was working, for she wasn't sure anything else would convince the board. She acknowledged that testimonials were likely to fall on deaf ears, but she was skeptical that anything else could be produced.

17. Radnor has only one middle school. If one wished to find the most comparable students for a possible control group comparison, the Welsh Valley or Balla Cynwyd Middle Schools in the Lower Merion Township School District, also in the west Philadelphia suburbs, would be the best bets. Or, might there be some way to relax temporarily the requirement that

all students in the middle school must go through the humanities curriculum, so that some might spend that time in the more traditional subject matter? That may not be feasible, but I need to probe this more. Without some sort of comparison, I worry that we might pick up student gains (or losses) and attribute them to the curriculum, whereas they really stem from maturation, or the "Classes for Youth" series on Channnel 7.

Author comments. These simulated conclusions are what I believe, reading between the lines, one might find if one spent a couple of days working in the Radnor School context. While these conclusions may be inaccurate, they represent the types of information that should be gleaned in an initial visit to a program. In one sense, the evaluation has already begun, and some of these conclusions represent evaluation findings. Yet many are still impressionistic and would need further confirmation before I would lean on them too heavily. For now, their primary utility would be to focus my design and further data collection efforts.

Without using space to comment on each item in my "memo," let me draw attention to two things.

First, specification of audiences for the evaluation findings is an essential, often neglected, part of evaluation design. Hopefully memo items 15 and 16 help make that point, if only on one dimension.

Second, item 17 alludes to the possibility of finding an appropriate comparison group. Space does not permit me to create enough of the context to outline in any sensible way what such a design might look like, for it could take many forms, dependent on the conditions. The specifics of the comparative design are less important here, however, than the fact that I would probably try to include a comparative element in any evaluation of a program such as this one. Such an approach can get to the heart of the issues of effectiveness and opportunity cost, where most other approaches are weaker or even speculative in this regard.

Both the comparative and noncomparative paradigms are well entrenched in educational evaluation and there is no unequivocal answer as to which is best for all evaluations. It obviously depends on the questions to be answered and the resources available for the evaluation, to mention only some of the determinants. What should be clear is that if one chooses, for whatever reason, to evaluate a program without looking at whether it produces the desired outcomes more efficiently or humanely than alternative programs (or no program at all), one never knows just what has been gained by choosing that particular program or lost by rejecting other, possibly better, alternatives.

Now, lest I be accused of falling prey to the "law of the instrument," let me hasten to note that I probably use a comparative evaluation design in less than half of the evaluations I conduct. Sometimes they simply are not feasible; sometimes they are irrelevant to the questions posed; sometimes I find it too much of an uphill struggle to disabuse educators of the widely held view that comparative experiments are irrelevant or harmful; and sometimes I'm simply not creative enough to come up with one that makes sense. But none of these facts dissuades me from the feeling that one should look carefully at the power of the comparative element in evaluation. Were this a real-life evaluation, I would work hard to see if a reasonable comparison could be included to get at issues such as relative effectiveness and cost of students spending time in the humanities curriculum versus other alternatives.

*   *   *

November 16. *Held a half-day meeting with Mrs. Janson, six other members of the curriculum committee, and the president of the board of education. Spent the first hour checking my perceptions about the program to make sure I was on track, but most of the meeting was devoted to discussing and resolving three issues.*

First, we talked at length about the polarization that seemed to be developing over the program and discussed the possibility of using an adversary evaluation approach in at least some parts of the study. That unnerved some of the group who felt there were too many adversaries as it was. I explained that I thought the approach had considerable merit when controversary already existed and opposing positions could be highlighted within the study rather than a battle waged around the evaluation. I explained that adversary evaluation attempts to assure fairness through seeking both positive and negative perspectives, that both sides of the issue should be illuminated, and that the range of information collected would tend to be broader. Equally important, critics would be much less likely to discount the evaluation as being biased. After some discussion of costs of collecting parallel information, we decided tentatively that the adversary approach might serve best in three ways: (a) plan to include the opinions of both strong supporters and detractors of the program—lay out the opposing points of view clearly and collect data insofar as possible to test these opposing claims; (b) enlist the aid of two well-selected evaluators, assign one to defend and one to attack the program, then have both review my evaluation design to see if additional data are needed to make their case as strong as possible; and (c) after the data are in, have my two colleagues review them and, as part of the final report, present and debate their cases, pro and con, on the basis of the evidence yielded by the study. Then the board can be the "jury" and reach a verdict. Not really the "adversary model" of evaluation, I admit, but the group resonated to some of those concepts from it and felt they would be helpful in ensuring fair play, plus being an excellent reporting technique. . .

Author comments. Some might suggest a more full-blown application of the adversary "model" of evaluation here, complete with opposing counsel, taking of testimony, cross-examination, and other accoutrements of the courtroom, possibly including a gavel and black-robed judge. While the latter is patently a pathetic parody, careful introduction and cross-examination of testimony can play a valuable role in many evaluations. Before I would commit the time and money necessary to set up a full-blown adversary trial or hearing for an educational program, however, I would ask whether there is a less cumbersome, equally valid way to get at the facts and opinions that witnesses might proffer, while maintaining the essence of what I view important in the adversarial approach. In this case, I think there is.

*   *   *

November 16 (continued). *Second, some of the teachers asked whether I really understood the program well enough to evaluate it. Would the program I evaluated really be their program, or my misconception of it. I suggested I write a description of the program and send it to Mrs. Janson. She and the humanities teachers could correct any errors in it, so we can reach agreement on just what it is that is being evaluated. . .*

Author comments. Why would I have the client review my written description of the program? Because of too many uncomfortable experiences of two types. First, my best efforts (and penetrating insight) not-withstanding, I have occasionally found late in an evaluation that I have not fully understood some basic aspects of the entity I was in the process of evaluating. As a result, I have had to scramble to patch a leaky evaluation design to keep the study afloat.

Even more troublesome are the infrequent instances when I understand the program perfectly well but, when the results are the least bit critical, program directors play an annoying variation of the shell game. Claims are made that the "program" evaluated is not the real program at all, and new descriptions different from those originally provided to the evaluator are offered as proof.

A simple remedy to both these problems is for me to write at the outset my best description of the program and its important elements, then provide that to the clients for their reaction, correction, rewriting—whatever it takes for them to agree and "sign-off" that the product of our joint effort represents an accurate description of their program. That keeps me from making foolish oversights or getting sandbagged by finding someone has moved the program since the data were collected. Personal preferences aside, I would recommend this step for virtually all evaluations, since it seems the epitome of arrogance to think one can evaluate adequately that which one cannot describe accurately.

*   *   *

November 16 (continued). *Finally, we spent the bulk of the time laying out the skeleton of an evaluation plan, which I suggested we do together. Some of the committee wanted the evaluation to focus on the curriculum goals and objectives, using those as organizers for collecting and reporting the data. But the board president noted that the objectives were really only part of the program, and she listed several important questions she felt would be overlooked if we were bound by the objectives. That was tremendous! It usually takes a fair bit of Rogerian counseling to get people to look beyond their written objectives, so I was quick to take the opportunity to tout the advantages of using evaluative questions as key organizers in an evaluation study. To illustrate, I put on the blackboard the questions I had gleaned over the past two days that they and others had said they would like the evaluation to answer. They got involved, started categorizing and collapsing questions, added others, and before we knew it, we had 17 evaluative questions that they all agreed should be dealt with in the study, plus a handful that were left in but viewed as lower in priority.*

With time running out, we took a few of the questions and, using a matrix I offered, went through the exercise of identifying information we would need to answer them, listing where and how we would obtain the information, and so on. It was great to see the enthusiasm of several of the group when they began to realize how simple and straightforward it was. Once they had the hang of it, I suggested they fill out as much of the matrix as they could for the remaining questions and then send it to me. I would try to refine it, flesh out the evaluation plan, and send it back to them for their final approval.

Didn't get the plan finished, but I feel good about what we were able to accomplish. More important, this isn't going to be my *evaluation plan, it is at least* ours, *if not* theirs, *built on questions they posed, and answered by information from sources they specified.*

Author comments. It is paramount to include representatives of all important audiences in the design of an evaluation study. Without that step, it is your evaluation design; with their involvement, there is an excellent chance they will see it as their design. What better way to have people come to understand evaluation and use its results than to get them involved as a partner in its conduct?

For me, an easy first step is to ask everyone directly or indirectly involved in the program what questions they would like to see answered by the evaluation study. Evaluators should feel free to inject their questions (and may need them for "pump-priming" so others get a feel for what is meant by "evaluative questions"), but a major portion of these questions should be drawn from those with a stake in the outcomes of the study.

Using questions (or objectives, if you prefer) as a springboard, I generally use a simple-minded, two-dimensional matrix to communicate to clients, funding agencies, report readers (and myself) how information is to be collected to answer each evaluative question. Jim Sanders and I evolved that matrix in our early joint evaluation work, and its seeds are contained in less pedestrian and explicit form in writings of several evaluators. It is embarrassingly simple but enormously useful.

*   *   *

December 3. *Received the draft of the Radnor group's effort to fill out the matrix for the remaining evaluative questions for their study. They got most of it filled out and had some interesting ideas I may not have thought of. Think I'll save a copy and use in my evaluation seminar to prove my point that much of evaluation planning,* sans *its mystique, is simple logic and should be shared by the client, with the evaluator providing technical help as and where it's needed.*

Author comments. Perusal of my handout for Spring quarter 1980 would reveal the document appearing as Artifact No. 3 on page 76, of which only a few samples are shown here in the interest of space.[6]

Yes, I do think it useful to have the client help identify possible sources of information, as well as possible ways to collect it. Methodological expertise notwithstanding, the evaluator seldom has the client's intimate feel for the program, who is really involved, who knows what, and even how certain groups or individuals might respond to proposed data collection techniques. Obviously the client should not be left to focus the evaluation alone, but there seems little reason for failure to involve the client as a partner at the design stage.

---

[6] Even these samples are only partial, providing the first four columns of a matrix. Subsequent columns which would need to be completed for each evaluative question (but omitted here to conserve space) include the following: arrangements for collecting information (by whom, when, under what conditions), analysis of information, and reporting of information (to whom, when, how).

Artifact No. 3. Sample Items from the Radnor Township Draft Evaluative Design

Evaluative Questions	Information Required	Source of Information	Strategy/Method of Collecting Information
1. To what extent are the program objectives shared by important groups?	Ratings of importance of objectives.	a. Board of education b. Hum. Curr. Review Comm. c. Teachers d. Parents e. Other community members	a-b. Individual interviews c-e. Mailed questionnaire survey to all teachers, samples of others, using Phi Delta Kappa Goal Ranking Procedure
2. To what degree does the curriculum address all the stated objectives?	Coverage of stated objectives in lesson plans and other materials.		
4. Is the content of the lesson plans faithful to the humanities?	Substantive adequacy of lessons and other materials.	a. Humanities faculty b. External humanities experts	a. Faculty analysis of curriculum, match to objectives b. Review/critique of faculty analysis above
		External humanities experts	Expert review of lesson plans and materials
5. Are social attitudes in the community such that the curriculum can be successfully implemented here at this time?	Attitudes of Community members and influence groups toward humanities.	a. Community members b. Community influence groups (for example, PTA and service club officers)	Mailed questionnaire survey to sample of community's citizens plus all identified "influence leaders"
9. Do the lesson plans and other curriculum materials use sound instructional theory?	Knowledge of instructional theory and methods.	Expert in instructional theory	Expert review of lesson plans and materials
13. Do student attitudes demonstrate that the curriculum is producing the desired results?	Attitudes of students toward the values and concepts taught in the curriculum.	Students	a. Comparative design, using attitude scales, observation, and unobstrusive measures; and? b. Simulated situations, role-playing to get at real student attitudes (for example, attitudes toward elderly, stereotyping of elderly)

A few comments about the matrix are in order. First, these sample evaluative questions do not pretend to be complete. Several key questions are obviously omitted, for example, questions about student learning of concepts presented in the curriculum.

Second, this simulated (but realistic) example of how the matrix might look obviously reflects a first draft in need of considerable refinement. Questions should be raised about whether other sources of information should be included or present sources excluded. Strategies for data collection and instruments are still vague in some instances and need to be checked for cost and feasibility.

Third, even when refined, there is no claim that this is the only way a good evaluation could be designed. I would claim, however, that it is a systematic way to produce a good evaluation design where the evaluator can assure it is technically sound while the client can be sure it is acceptable on other grounds.

Finally, the matrix contains "pieces" of the evaluation which still need to be summarized to yield the real evaluation design. For example, summarizing the columns on methods and arrangements for collecting information will normally identify several questions to be posed to the same source (for instances, teachers), using the same method (such as a mailed questionnaire). Economy of time and effort (and the respondent's patience) will generally result from collecting all the information in a single instrument. Such summarization also quickly reveals inconsistencies and infeasible proposals in the draft.

*   *   *

December 6. *Completed the evaluation design for the Radnor humanities curriculum today. In the process, I realized we had never explicitly agreed on the standards or criteria the board would use in determining whether or not to continue the program, even though we had discussed them in relationship to the evaluative questions and I had talked individually with some board members about them. So I called Mrs. Reese, the board president, and asked her if she might be able to help me with that. We agreed she should go to her colleagues on the board with the list of evaluative questions and ask them, "What kind of answer to this question would convince you to continue the program? To discontinue it?" Given answers to those questions, we can list some pretty explicit criteria that will help me decide what emphasis to place on the various kinds of data.*

Author comments. There are many ways one might go about setting criteria for determining whether an entity like this humanities curriculum should be continued or jettisoned. The example offered here is admittedly somewhat tardy if you believe that the only criteria of importance are those held by the formal decision makers. Yet I find formal decision makers seldom work in a vacuum and are often influenced by what standards other groups use to judge the program. Once I tended to blurt out, within moments of an introductory handshake with a decision maker, "OK, now what criteria do you intend to use to determine whether or not to continue the program?" I am now more patient. Indeed, I like to share the full range of questions various groups hold to be important with the formal decision makers—in this case the board—and ask them, in essence, whether the answer to that question would influence them to continue or scrap the program. Not only can one generate criteria in this way, but there is also the possibility of expanding the horizons of those who must make difficult decisions.

*   *   *

December 13. *Mrs. Reese called back today after polling the board members on criteria. She reported that she and one other member of the board think all the questions should be used to decide whether to keep the humanities curriculum. But consensus of the board is that the most important criteria relate to three areas: (1) how well students are performing in basic skills (writing and other language skills); (2) whether students are attaining the general and specific goals of the curriculum (critical thinking, appreciation of cultural, ethnic, and social diversity); and (3) whether the patrons of the school wish to see the curriculum continued. With that information, I can complete the evaluation plan and send a copy off to Mrs. Janson tomorrow.*

Author comments. Mrs. Reese may not have reported formalized criteria, per se, but she has given the stuff of which criteria are made. I have nothing against decision makers who tell me they intend to continue a program only if "the mean score of students exceeds the 74th percentile on the vocabulary section of the ITBS," just so long as they can defend their rationale and chosen instrument. Conversely, I have a great deal against the arbitrariness that typically underlies such statements. I would much rather have a glimmer of what decision makers really think important (and some future opportunity to help them reflect more specifically on how they intend to apply the criteria) than to deal with the artificial precision built into too many of today's so-called criteria.

*   *   *

December 14. *Completed the Radnor evaluation plan tonight. Was disappointed to find I had to cut out some things I feel are important* *because there simply isn't enough time and/or money to do them. Alas. Still, I think the plan is a good one, given the constraints we're operating under.*

Artifact No. 4

Outline of the Humanities Program Evaluation

I. Introduction
   A. History and Description of the Humanities Curriculum
   B. Purposes of the Evaluation
   C. Audiences for Evaluation
   D. Constraints and Policies Within Which the Evaluation Must Operate

II. Evaluation plan
   A. Overview
      1. Possible comparative elements
      2. Planned opposition: use of the adversary evaluation approach
      3. Sequencing and interrelationship of components
      4. Evaluative questions to be addressed by the study
      5. Criteria for judging the program
   B. Work Unit 1.0; Curriculum Analysis
      1. Expert review: humanities specialists
      2. Expert review: instructional design specialist
   C. Work Unit 2.0; Collection of Extant Data
      1. Existing records
      2. Unobtrusive measures
   D. Work Unit 3.0: Mailed Questionnaire Surveys
      1. Survey populations/samples
      2. Survey instruments
      3. Follow-up techniques
      4. Nonresponse bias checks
   E. Work Unit 4.0: Student Measures
      1. Cognitive measures
         a. Basic skills
         b. Humanities content
      2. Affective measures
         a. Attitude scales
         b. Simulated situation: role-playing
   F. Work Unit 5.0: Evaluation Team On-site Visit
      1. Classroom observation
      2. Interviews
         a. Students
         b. Teachers

        c. Parents
        d. Board members

III. Reporting of results
    A. Preliminary Report: Exit Interview of On-site Team
    B. Final Report and Executive Summary
    C. Review of Draft Reports
    D. Debating the Pros and Cons

IV. Personnel
    A. External Evaluation Team
    B. Radnor Staff (Supervised Participation)

V. Schedule
    A. Work Flow
    B. Deadlines

VI. Budget

Author comments. Space prohibits commentary on each of the points in this sketchy outline of the plan, but elaboration may be helpful on a few points that may not be self-evident.

First, for reasons outlined earlier, I would try to get comparative snapshots of the students in the program and other comparable youngsters on variables outlined in work units II-C and II-E. Without more information about the availability of other comparison groups and willingness to allow their use, one could only temporize at this stage, laying out a possible comparative design in II-A and promising, should that prove infeasible, to direct the resources assigned to that effort into more intensive data collection within Radnor on those variables.

Second, within each "work unit" proposed, I would preview *briefly* the type of instrument I would use (listing specific instruments if they are already in existence) and the proposed data analysis.

Third, in work unit 1.0, I would propose sending program goals and lesson plans to the appropriate experts and have them conduct their analyses from afar, unsullied by the rhetoric of the enthusiastic program staff. If resources did not stretch far enough to cover the day or two of consultant time needed here, one could have appropriately selected members of the on-site evaluation team complete this task.

Fourth, in work unit 2.0, I would envision collection of information on variables such as instances of in-school problems among different ethnic groups, membership in elective dance, drama, or art classes, museum attendance, and the like.

Fifth, in work unit 4.0, I would probably depend on a combination of criterion and norm-referenced measures to get at the basic skills. In addition, I would want to sample students' written products, given the emphasis the curriculum places on that area. In the humanities content, local criterion-referenced measures should be constructed, working co-operatively with the humanities faculty to make certain the items reflect important concepts. In addition, I would want to select a good measure of critical thinking to get at those ambitious program goals.

In the affective area, I would again work closely with teachers to design self-report scales that would assess student attitudes (such as "appreciation" and "sensibility") toward the various content areas. As a supplement, I would structure simulated situations and role playing opportunities where a smaller sample of students could react directly to stimuli, making choices that reveal relevant attitudes (for instance, stereotypic perceptions of the elderly).

Sixth, I would use an intensive on-site visit of two or three days duration as one of the major sources of data. For all its limitations, there is a great deal to be said for good old-fashioned professional judgment by those who know the territory. So I would be certain to include both humanities experts and evaluation specialists on a team of four or five persons. With careful advance scheduling, orientation of the team to the evaluative questions and the interview schedules, splitting the team up to conduct individual interviews, and then coming back to debrief and synthesize findings, a good bit can be accomplished in a reasonably short time (if the team survives the inhumane pace).

Seventh, once the instruments and instructions for their use were completed, I would rely heavily on Radnor district staff to assist with much of the on-site data collection and tabulation, thus greatly amplifying the data that can be collected on a small evaluation budget. The cynic might worry that anxiety over the results could lead to embellishment of these data, but that seems a small risk if one builds in spot checks at each step of data collection and coding.

Finally, this evaluation plan proposes what might be called an eclectic, "multiple-source, multiple-method" evaluation, with all the advantages claimed earlier in this chapter for such an approach. It also incorporates where appropriate the adversary approach, in ways outlined earlier in the journal entry for November 16. But is the plan really any good? That brings us to the next point.

* * *

December 19. *With yesterday being the last day of classes, I went back over the Radnor evaluation design to see how it stacked up on the*

11 general meta-evaluation criteria I've advocated.[7] *Using the 11 criteria as a starting point, I rated it (unbiasedly, of course) as follows.*

1. Conceptual Clarity. Fairly good, *given the sections on purposes of the study, the use of adversary and comparative elements, and how the components fit together. Should have been more explicit about the summative nature of the study, however.*

2. Characterization of the Object of the Evaluation. Excellent, *as judged by the humanities department head, who edited my written program description, and then "certified" it as accurate.*

3. Recognition and Representation of Legitimate Audiences. Good, *since I identified what everyone agrees to be the major audiences (and am collecting data from each of them as well). I was not clear in my section on reporting on plans for transmitting the final results to the various audiences, however. Change the gold star to silver.*

4. Sensitivity to Political Problems in the Evaluation. Good, *largely due to: (1) the advantages of the adversary "pro and con" reports; (2) clarity and agreements about the policies within which the evaluation will be conducted; (3) the use of humanities experts to assure that relevant content expertise will be applied; and (4) the comfort the humanities staff has taken in knowing they will see a draft of the final report before it "goes to press."*

5. Specification of Information Needs and Sources. Excellent. *Here is where the matrix (and a compulsive-obsessive personality) pay off.*

6. Comprehensiveness/Inconclusiveness. Excellent. *Drawing evaluative questions from all the groups, plus tossing in some of my own, resulted in an array of variables that I believe represents a very comprehensive set. If something is happening in that humanities program, we will spot it.*

7. Technical Adequacy. ? *Too early to tell. The recipe looks sound enough, but the real "proof of the pudding" is still in the future. It is easier to describe instruments to be constructed than to construct them so they meet acceptable technical specifications.*

8. Consideration of Costs. Poor. *I really missed the boat here. Having ascertained the dollar cost of the program earlier and having talked a lot about opportunity costs, I didn't make my intentions for handling either of these very explicit in the plan itself. I need to rectify that.*

9. Explicit Standards/Criteria. Good. *They are there, but some may not feel they are explicit enough as stated. I think they communicate.*

10. Judgments and/or Recommendations. ? *To me, making judgments*

---

[7] See B. R. Worthen, "Characteristics of a Good Evaluation Study," *Journal of Research and Development in Education* 10 (Spring 1977): 3-20.

and recommendations is an integral part of the role I play as an evaluator. But I never say much about that at the design stage—I just do it automatically when it comes time to report. Maybe that should be clearer in the evaluation plan so the client knows what to expect.

11. Reports Tailored to Audiences. Fair. *I noted that there would be (1) an omnibus technical evaluation report that self-consciously includes all the details, and (2) a short executive summary of major findings, using nontechnical language and graphs (in place of tabular presentation of data analyses). That was tossed off too quickly, however, with little thought about whether all audiences would find one or the other of those reports appropriate; whether there should be an oral presentation to the board, complete with multicolored overheads; and a one-page summary in case the press wants to run something. I need to think more about this long before we get to the reporting stage.*

Author comments. Evaluations are often designed (mine, at least) under pressure of deadlines. I would like in my lifetime to design an evaluation where I had sufficient time to build the design, carefully cross-checking each part for compliance with criteria that I and others view as touchstones of a good evaluation. Instead, I generally find myself wondering, after I have completed the design, if it really meets those standards of a good evaluation. I hope that after some years of worrying about them, those standards have become second nature and their consideration instinctive at each stage of the work. Realistically, unless one suffers delusions of grandeur, it seems safer to check one's plan against any of the extant lists of meta-evaluation criteria. They might be as simple as the one used here or as comprehensive as the recently published evaluation standards that took half a decade or more in their development.[8] At the design stage, I care less about which set of criteria is applied than I do about the fact that time is taken for careful review of the design to see if there are critical flaws or omissions.

*   *   *

December 21. *Mrs. Janson called today and indicated the board and committee had given the go-ahead on the plan I submitted, with the only suggested change coming in the deadline. The board has decided they cannot delay a decision about the humanities curriculum until next year, as they had orginally planned. Instead, they want to make a decision by*

---

[8] Joint Committee on Standards for Educational Evaluation, *Standards for Evaluation of Educational Programs, Projects, and Materials* (New York: McGraw-Hill Book Company, 1981).

March 15 so they will have time, should they decide to discontinue the program, to plan for its phase-out and provision of alternative curricular offerings for the students.

That disappoints me, for it forces me to withdraw; there is simply no way I can free enough time to develop the instruments, supervise the data collection, coordinate the on-site visit, and orchestrate the expert reviews of the materials by that deadline. I recommended several colleagues who could do an excellent job of carrying out the design we had developed. Mrs. Janson agreed to contact them to see about a replacement to undertake the actual evaluation.

Fortunately, most of the design can still be implemented and completed within their deadline, although it will be tight. The greatest problem this new deadline causes is the loss of any chance to look at changes in students over time—something I had intended with the cognitive, affective, and unobtrusive measures of student behavior. That weakens the evaluation, but hopefully the combination of perspectives left in the study will still be strong enough to yield solid findings.

Well, good luck to whoever ends up doing this evaluation.

Author comments. The best laid plans of mice and evaluators, to paraphrase, seldom work smoothly. (That is why evaluators need to be not only intellectually flexible but also emotionally robust.) It is not uncommon for deadlines to be abruptly shifted for reasons far less reasonable than that which I invented as the rationale of the Radnor board. Let me strike one last blow for eclectic, multiple-method evaluation designs; they are considerably more robust to changes than are their more single-minded counterparts. If one facet of the multiple-method design is lost because of new circumstances that make it infeasible, the evaluation may limp a little, but it can almost always carry on to yield data the decision maker needs. If one depends on a single strategy for collecting information and it so happens that changing circumstances disrupt that strategy, there is much less likelihood that the evaluation will succeed.

Having the board change their timelines and cause me to withdraw from the evaluation is, however, less an instructional point than an artifice to terminate these interminable journal entries and bring this chapter to a close. Tracing our evaluation hero through instrument development, data collection, analysis, reporting, and recuperation phases of the evaluation would double the length of this chapter—so some graceful exit is required.

Perhaps there is little real loss in foregoing the journal entries that would have paralleled the actual conduct of the evaluation, because activities for each step are foreshadowed in the plan, and the reader should readily be able to leap the gap to how the real activity would be conducted. In closing, I would like to comment on a few areas where subtleties or potential snags might slow or derail the evaluation if not handled correctly.

Conducting the Evaluation

There is one dangling detail that should be mentioned as a precursor to conducting the evaluation: finalizing the agreement between evaluator and client. The evaluation plan provides a good basis for this, but there should be some form of written agreement or letter of understanding that incorporates the plan, agrees on reporting deadlines, budget, and the like. I would urge development of such an agreement in virtually any significant evaluation enterprise. Some may see seeds of distrust in such urging. I agree, but the distrust is not of the motives or character of the principal parties; it is merely distrust of their total recall of an understanding made months earlier.

In larger evaluation studies, one may wish for a more formal contractual arrangement. Guidelines for what to include in such a contract (as well as suggestions for how to identify a well-qualified evaluator) have been written elsewhere[9] and will not be repeated here.

Selecting or Designing Evaluation Instruments

Were I to conduct this evaluation, I would turn quickly to Buros' *Mental Measurement Yearbooks* or other collections that may contain well-developed instruments relevant to some of the data-collection needs. Even though I am never too optimistic about finding just the right instrument, I suspect useful instruments on variables such as critical thinking, writing and language arts, and attitudes toward different cultural groups and ethnicity could be located in these sources.

Even if one did not find usable instruments, there is a high probability of finding useful strategies and formats for asking questions that will make instrument design an easier task.

Where no instruments exist—and I suspect that would be the case for most of the specific content of the humanities curriculum—home-made (do not misread that as carelessly made) cognitive measures would need to be fashioned. How to construct those with an eye to validity and other

---

[9] W. J. Wright and B. R. Worthen, *Standards and Procedures for Evaluation Contracting* (Portland, Ore.: Northwest Regional Educational Laboratory, 1975).

technical considerations is another day's tale. Suffice it to say here that I would work closely with the humanities faculty and members of the humanities study committee in designing those instruments. That not only assures relevance, but it also is an excellent way to build rapport and trust with those whose program is being evaluated. I would also pilot drafts of the resulting criterion-referenced instruments with small samples of students. The strategy for designing affective measures would be similar.

Although student measures are often viewed as the most difficult to construct, the most poorly designed instruments in most educational evaluations are usually questionnaires or interview schedules. If one traces the professional genealogy of most educational evaluators, their parentage is frequently found to consist of educational and psychological methodologists. Small wonder that our evaluators seem to have inherited an ancestral sneer toward mailed questionnaire surveys or interview studies. Most educational and psychological methodologists have long misunderstood (or worse, never studied) the data-collection methods and strategies of the sociometrician, and are more likely to mistake Kornhauser and Sheatsley for a law firm rather than recognizing them as authors of a very useful set of guidelines for designing good mailed questionnaires.[10] Rather than expanding on a pet peeve here, let me simply indicate that the design of good questionnaires and interview schedules is a task that demands every bit as much time and creativity as the design of more traditional cognitive and affective measures.

Collecting the Information

Most of the information collection activities can be readily inferred from the evaluation plan outline, but two elaborations may be helpful.

First, it is important to capitalize on what is known about survey methods if one intends to obtain an adequate response rate to a mailed questionnaire. There exists a body of literature on how to increase response rates. In addition, it would be important to know and use appropriate techniques for assessing whether respondents and nonrespondents differ significantly on relevant variables that might bias the results.

Second, little has been said about observation within classrooms; yet I would see that as a pivotal part of the study. Here I would want the humanities specialist(s) to accompany me, or perhaps take the lead. The

---

[10] A. Kornhauser and P. Sheatsley, "Questionnaire Construction and Interview Procedures," in *Research Methods in Social Relations,* edited by C. Selltiz and others (New York: Holt, 1959).

evaluator should be able to get a fairly good feel for the classroom climate, the effectiveness of the instruction, whether the curriculum objectives were being translated into learning activities fôr students, and how students react to those activities. The humanities expert is needed, however, to get at the more subtle nuances to judge whether what students are learning in the classroom is really the essence of what is important for them to know about the humanities.

Reporting the Evaluation Findings

Few evaluation reports hold such general interest that they are media events. In contexts like the Radnor humanities curriculum, however, several individuals and groups will generally press to get a preview of the findings at the earliest possible moment. The more visible the evaluation, the more curious the local folk get about the outcomes. When outside experts begin roaming through, requests for evaluation findings often spring up in their wake.

In the Radnor case, I would probably restrict early release of information to the previously mentioned exit interview at the conclusion of the on-site evaluation visit. This is a natural and expected time to share at least general impressions of the evaluation team. The audiences for that report (probably the humanities staff, the principal, and representatives of the humanities committee and the board) should be reminded that this is only one facet of the evaluation, and that the results of the on-site evaluation will have to be integrated with those from the other evaluation activities into a more comprehensive report before they will have the full picture that the evaluation will provide.

In preparing the final report, I would produce a complete first draft including at least the following:

1. An introduction describing the humanities curriculum, purposes and audiences for the evaluation, and an overview of the rest of the report.

2. Listing of the evaluative questions used to guide the study.

3. Overview of the evaluation plan, with a supporting appendix to provide detail. (The matrix described earlier is often a helpful inclusion in the overview section of the plan.)

4. Discussion of findings, probably organized around the evaluative questions. (Again, detailed presentations of findings generated by each instrument could be provided in an appendix.)

5. Recommendations, with sufficient rationale and linkage to findings to demonstrate that the recommendations are warranted.

Once completed, I would submit the draft copy of the report to the principal and ask that she review it and also have it reviewed by the head of the humanities faculty, other selected members of the humanities study committee, and the board president. The intent of this review would be twofold: first, to identify any factual inaccuracies; and second, to challenge any inferences, conclusions, or recommendations these partisan reviewers think are inappropriate, unwarranted, or unfair. It is important, in asking for these reviews, to communicate that you will take them very seriously and will consider carefully each suggested revision, whether it be minor editing or deletion of a major recommendation. It is equally important to make very clear that the ultimate decision for what goes into the final report draft belongs to the evaluator, and that there is no guarantee that all of their suggestions will be incorporated. Failure to get these groundrules clear at the outset can lead to all manner of problems.[11]

Having the client review a draft of the report and vouchsafe its factual accuracy is good insurance against the evaluator committing serious blunders. Helpful clients have saved me embarrassment by correcting nontrivial errors I failed to spot in draft reports (like the "typo" that turned a K-3 program into K-8, or the instance when I described a project director as single-minded, but the typewriter rendered it "simple-minded").

Even small factual errors, uncorrected, give comfort to the critic bent on discrediting the report. Consider, for instance, the PTA president who had opposed a new curriculum designed to teach reading through a study of local cultures, only to find that our evaluation showed clearly that the curriculum was having a very positive effect on student learning. "How," he thundered at a collective PTA and school board meeting, "can you believe anything else is accurate if the evaluator can't even spell the name of the school or its principal right!" (Now before you judge too harshly, *you* should try to evaluate the curriculum at Tchesinkut School, where Mr. Nakinilerak presides.) It was there in the Alaskan bush that I first learned the value of asking clients to review and share responsibility for accuracy of the final report.

Several references have been made previously to an executive summary. This might take the form of a parsimonious introductory chapter to the evaluation report, including a synopsis of the findings, plus references to other sections of the report of interest to particular audiences. Or, the executive summary might be a separate, self-contained document of five to ten pages for use with interested parties who need to know the results

---

11 Mitch Brickell has described a number of these problems (including the client who insists on final editing of the evaluator's report) in his delightful paper, "The Influence of External Political Factors on the Role and Methodology of Evaluation," *Research, Evaluation and Development Paper No. 7* (Portland, Ore.: Northwest Regional Educational Laboratory, 1975).

but are not concerned with details. In larger evaluations, where more people need to be informed, a brief evaluation abstract of one or two pages might be useful.

One ethical consideration that should not be neglected in report writing is preserving desired confidentiality and anonymity. Evaluators generally promise that individual responses or test scores will not be divulged (except with the individuals' express approval). Unfortunately, that promise is sometimes forgotten at the report-writing stage.

Finally, there is the matter of the adversary debate promised as part of the final report. Space permits only the following comments:[12]

1. Presentation of the pros and cons of a program might well take the standard debate form of presentations and rebuttals. The same format could be extended to written debates concerning the merits of the program.

2. Careful groundrules and arbiters need to be set in advance so that, in the heat of "adversarying," collegial congeniality does not give way to opponents making disparaging remarks about one another's mothers.

3. Every effort should be made to keep in mind (*everyone's* mind, even the two adversaries) that the evaluation is a search for truth, not an arena for winning at all costs. It alters the ethics of evaluation if one or both adversaries feel compelled to beat the opposition, even if the data are strained or ignored in the process. I believe the appropriate mandate in this instance would be that of presenting the most positive and negative cases that can be made for the Radnor humanities curriculum *on the basis of existing evidence,* rather than constructing potent but specious arguments that depend more on polemics than on plain facts.

Conclusion

We have reached the end of the chapter, yet I have only scratched the surface of what actually happens in carrying out any real evaluation. Most evaluation studies are complex and comprehensive enterprises. Beneath the complexity, however, lie many simple, straightforward steps on which the evaluator and client can work as partners. I hope my imaginary evaluation has been instructive on some of those practical guidelines. Finally, evaluation studies are strongest, in my opinion, when tailored specifically to meet the client's needs, drawing as necessary on multiple perspectives rather than following the prescriptions of any one

---

[12] For a more complete treatment of how such debates might be conducted, the reader is referred to B. R. Worthen and W. T. Rogers, "The Pitfalls and Potential of Adversary Evaluation," *Educational Leadership* 37 (April 1980): 536-543.

evaluation model or method. It would be disappointing if my contrived evaluation failed to make that point.

I must confess that writing this chapter has been therapeutic. It is the only evaluation I have ever conducted from the comfort of my arm-chair, and it is the only evaluation where no one has raised questions about my design or my motives, or even my ancestry. Yes indeed, doing these make-believe evaluations could prove addictive.

8.
Groping for the Elephant

by Henry M. Brickell

Henry M. Brickell is a former middle school student, high school teacher, school district administrator, professor, and dean, as well as the father of four public school students. His other qualifications for writing this chapter include directing 100 evaluation studies for local, state, and national education agencies. He is Director, Policy Studies in Education, New York City.

There are more things in evaluation, Horatio, than are dreamt of in your philosophy. It starts earlier, reaches further, stops later, and helps more than you dream.

* * *

In the fable about the four blind men and the elephant, the blind men each learned something about the elephant, but presumably nothing about themselves. The elephant learned something about blind men, but presumably nothing about elephants. In contrast, we—the outsiders—can learn some things about the Radnor elephant, some things about the evaluators, some things about their groping, and some things about the habitat of elephants.

First, what do we learn about the Radnor humanities *program?* That it exists in the eye of the beholder, invisible except in reflection. The actual humanities program, or whatever it is, is less important than what people think it is. That becomes the primary reality—and even the data—determining what will happen to it. The reason for perceptions overriding other realities is touched on later.

Second, what do we learn about evaluators as *people?* That it matters which one you hire. They come in through different doors, go through different motions, and go out through different windows (or through the roof, Michael).

If they were doctors, one would declare the patient hearty in the waiting room; some would call for days of testing; and one would pronounce the patient dead on arrival. If lawyers, one would call the case lost; one won; many in doubt. Is this as true for evaluators as for doctors and lawyers? Yes. I wish our profession were more data-based than theirs, but it isn't.

A school administrator telephoned me once: "Mitch, since we're friends, I'll be direct. Do you sell endorsements?" I didn't, but someone else did, and my friend went elsewhere. That was back before I diversified.

Third, what do we learn about evaluation *techniques?* That they have the power to assess everything from goals to outcomes, starting before the program does and ending after the program does. They are remarkably diverse: some are derived from models and some not; some are pre-planned and some not; some are objective and some not. They offer every method of data collection from observation to tests, and every method of data analysis from case study to statistical tests. Some are preferred by some evaluators and some by others.

Fourth, what do we learn about the *territories* in which evaluations are conducted? That every one is different, but they have a lot in common. And what they have in common—pressures from people who often hold strong opinions and who care about the evaluation results—is frequently not pleasant.

The Program

Like you, the seven evaluators know the program only in print (plus a handful of phone calls to Radnor). Here is what I say about what they say about what Radnor says about the program.

1. Goals aren't guarantees.

Like used car salespersons, educators can claim anything while the program is still standing on the lot. There is something about walking under the flapping flags and blinding floodlights that brings out the hyper-bole in a man. What is the best the thing might conceivably do with Andretti at the wheel? Forget the sawdust in the transmission; let's talk Watkins Glen.

There is something about a blank sheet of white paper with the word "Goals" at the top that intoxicates a curriculum committee. Forget the teachers' abilities, adolescent kids, and two periods a week; let's talk the human condition. Claim a lot or they won't buy it. Claim a lot more and they won't measure it.

Neither the profession nor the public exacts a penalty for high ambi-tion. So shoot the moon. Else what is heaven for, etc. The other players will so thrill to your bravery they won't make you count the points in your hand when you lose. Well, most players won't.

Popham: As a consequence of two classes per week, it is expected that students will increase their aesthetic sensibilities, critical thinking skills, appreciation of human achievement in the arts, appreciation of their own and others' cultural heritages, understanding of the interrelatedness among disparate disciplines—not to mention their communication skills. . . . In contrast, the cleric's task of spiriting folks through the Pearly Gates seems fairly modest.

Eisner: It takes more than a little guts these days to attempt to develop a program in the humanities for adolescents. The push in most school districts is for a larger dose of the Three R's. Yet students should have access to important ideas about the nature of man; educational goals should include quality of experience as well as measurable competencies. American education would do well to have more such programs.

Scriven: There are excellent reasons for a curriculum that address the general issues about the nature of humanity, which this curriculum is supposed to address. There are no reasons from the lesson topic list to think that this curriculum addresses them. . . . Locally-designed curriculums, like locally-constructed tests, are about on a par with home-brewed medicine—once in a while you get lucky, but most of the time you get sick, and in this case, it is your children who suffer. They need strong medicine and a sound diet; this is soda pop and junk food.

2. Humanities are incomparable.

Long ago, back in 1970, evaluators worried about whether programs achieved their objectives. That was enough to give them Excedrin headache #1. More recently, say in 1975, they worried about whether there was a better program for achieving the same objectives. Headache #2. Today, they worry about whether there are better objectives standing around the schoolyard that could be brought into the classrooms and achieved instead. Headache #3.

Underlying this shift is a growing recognition of a concept borrowed from economics: opportunity cost. Simply expressed, it means: could I make more money this afternoon by doing something besides writing this chapter? (Yes. Anything.) Applied to Radnor, it means: could the kids be taught something more important than humanities? Radnor teachers have tried to make the answer negative by putting every available objective into the program so there will be nothing else kids could be taught.

Listen to the evaluators fret about whether the humanities in Radnor are incomparable.

Stake/Pearsol: Jim suggested the evaluation might consider "opportunity costs"—what other learnings or student experiences are overshadowed or ignored by continuing the humanities program.

Bonnet: If [the program is] dropped, something else will have to take place during those four hours per week in each student's schedule. This realization changes many of the evaluation questions from absolute ones (How good is the program?) to comparative ones (How good is the program compared to what would replace it?).

Scriven: Abolish the program, as soon as possible, regardless of whether it is replaced by another "humanities" program, basics, or bicycle-riding. . . I do not claim that nothing valuable is being acquired from any of the lessons. The alternative to this humanities program is not a sensory deprivation tank. The curriculum is indefensible unless its effects are *enormously better* than the same amount of time spent on assigned reading. That's the zero comparison level, because that involves (roughly) a saving of four salaried professional positions.

The People

Like you, the seven evaluators are not blind; but, like you, they are human. Here we see them in all their humanity—feet of clay, and so forth.

3. Evaluators know their world, not yours.

Radnor, like other schools, has three distinct choices: (1) hire subject matter experts who do not know evaluation and have them supplement themselves with evaluation expertise; (2) hire evaluation experts and have them do the reverse; or (3) hire hybrids who know both the subject matter and evaluation. For this book, ASCD made the second and third choices.

The third choice would seem at first glance to contain the best of both worlds, but it can give you evaluators who already know the evaluation answers because they know the subject matter questions. Take Scriven, who has an excellent background in philosophy as well as in evaluation and avoids Radnor with an initial unfavorable opinion. Or take Eisner, who has an excellent background in the arts as well as in evaluation and approaches Radnor with an initial favorable opinion. Perhaps Eisner's extensive knowledge of the arts has led him to develop unusually clear aesthetic values and has made him unusually sensitive to similar values espoused by the Radnor program.

Eisner: Education is not a neutral enterprise. A neutral evaluator would not know how to begin or what to look for.

The second choice—have evaluation experts supplement themselves with subject matter expertise—is the one Worthen offers when his disguise slips off and we see him for the evaluator he is.

> **Worthen:** One [humanities teacher] asked how anyone except an expert in humanities could presume to evaluate a humanities curriculum. I countered by pointing out that I write doggerel, publish an occasional short story, and once even tried to sell an oil painting. He wasn't easily impressed . . . the discovery that the evaluator is not a specialist in the content or process at the heart of the program being evaluated is often a rude shock to the client . . . I used to try to convert clients with repeated and lengthy appeals to reason. Experience (and exhaustion) have convinced me of the wisdom of eschewing such appeals in favor of simple promises to obtain judgments of relevant substantive experts as part of the evaluation.

4. Evaluators don't walk on water.

There is much common sense in these chapters, but not much uncommon sense. Any mystery comes not from magic, but from jargon, and there is, happily, little of that. There is not much here—or elsewhere in evaluation—that the ordinary professional couldn't do, if it were in plain English, except sit through meetings of the Evaluation Research Society, which are not in plain English. Take these simple steps as an example:

> **Bonnet:** 1. Learn more about the program and the setting.
> 2. Identify decision makers and their perspectives.
> 3. List all the purposes, audiences, and questions the study might reasonably address.
> 4. Outline various methods for answering the proposed questions.
> 5. Decide which questions to pursue.
> 6. Complete the evaluation plan.
> 7. Collect and analyze data.
> 8. Report the findings.

Like doctors who ask you where it hurts, barbers who ask how you want it cut, architects who ask where you want it put, and painters who ask what color you want it, evaluators ask you to supply all of the information they need. You have to tell them what questions to answer, where to go for the answers, and what the answers are. And eventually you have to decide what to do about the answers.

> **Webster:** . . . the evaluator would meet with the committee to generate a list of critical decisions to be made concerning the program, to de-

termine the types of information necessary to make those decisions, and to plan the informational sources in such a way that critical decisions would be precipitated by timely and objective information.

Worthen: For me, an easy first step is to ask everyone directly or indirectly involved in the program what questions they would like to see answered by the evaluation study.

5. Evaluators walk on eggs.

As a rule, evaluators are quite sensitive to the interpersonal environments where they work. They take care to find out whose values, reputations, or jobs are at stake and to be responsive to the personal feelings of the people involved. Evaluators know they are engaged in a human enterprise as well as a technical exercise.

After all, evaluation is an art, making it one of the humanities and evaluators humanists.

Popham: . . . I've learned via a score of hard-knock experiences that the quality of interpersonal relationships between evaluator, evaluatee, and decision makers is crucial. I'd work darned hard to establish relationships of trust between me and the other parties in the endeavor.

Bonnet: I'd begin with a long talk with the person who invited me into this battle. . . . My work would end just as it began: with a long talk with the principal. This time she'd get my congratulations or condolences along with whatever advice I could offer on her next challenge—to execute the board's decision with authority and grace.

This rule, like others, of course has its exceptions.

Scriven: Isn't all this very *mean?* No, it's either true or false. Truth telling is the professional task of the evaluator, not being a friend or parent or PR representative. *Should* anyone be this mean? Yes; in this context.

But even here, what we are seeing is Scriven's humane concern for young minds overriding his concern for adult sensibilities.

The Techniques

Evaluators have whole books of recipes for cooking up assessments. But most of them don't cook by the book; they use a pound of this and a pinch of that, sniffing and tasting as they go, and often wind up slightly surprised at the way they did it.

6. Nobody lives in a model house.

All the chapter authors were asked to use their model, or someone else's model, to evaluate Radnor—more exactly, to think through how Radnor should be evaluated. Only Webster explicates the model he is using, CIPP, although Stake/Pearsol guide their thinking by Stake's own "responsive" model of evaluation. All the others eschew models. (Scriven grinds the program between his teeth.)

What is an evaluation model? Every evaluation model is an abstraction based on an abstraction, a generalized plan for assessing a generalized program. The strength of every model is in its grasp of the general, the common; the weakness of every model is in its missing of the particular, the uncommon. Most of the chapter authors believe that Radnor is an uncommon case requiring the creation of a special design, not the application of a general design.

Webster, doing what ASCD asked, tries to move the Radnor family into the CIPP model house. This causes some strain because the Radnors have been living together in the forest for some time without benefit of an evaluation ceremony. Stake, doing what ASCD asked, and responsive architect that he is, designs a tent to fit the Radnor family. No strain. The other evaluators, responding to Radnor without a responsive model to guide them, do the same. (Scriven leaves the Radnor family to freeze in the snow.)

> **Webster:** The CIPP model identifies four major types of evaluation: context evaluation to feed planning decisions; input evaluation to feed programming decisions; process evaluation to feed implementing decisions; and product evaluation to feed recycling decisions.

> **Stake/Pearsol:** What Jim and Bob tried to accomplish was a review of the humanities curriculum as it was perceived by the key individuals associated with it. . . . By responding to the concerns of the various constituencies, they provided a responsive evaluation report.

> **Worthen:** . . . I am a self-confessed eclectic in my own evaluation work, designing each evaluation *de novo*, using pieces of the so-called "models" only if they seem relevant and appropriate. . . . I find greater relevance in tailoring by "snipping and sewing" together bits and pieces off the more traditional ready-mades and even weaving a bit of homespun, if necessary, to cover the client's needs.

> **Popham:** There's precious little allure in referring to something as Popham's Model. I suppose I could abbreviate it, but the initials P.M. have already been staked out by those who like to tell time. Perhaps I could try Popham's Procedure, but that abbreviation is even worse. . . . Hence, please don't think of what follows as an attempt to describe a formal evaluation model.

7. There are different gropes from different folks.

Readers won't miss the ideas that appear in chapter after chapter—or if they did, they could probably think them up themselves—ideas like these:

1. Get a signed contract that explains the responsibilities of both parties.
2. Ask everyone what he or she wants to know.
3. Confirm the goals and objectives.
4. Collect several kinds of evidence from several sources.
5. Examine teaching as well as learning.
6. Look for unintended effects.
7. Write several reports for different audiences and purposes. Let Radnor correct factual errors, but retain final control over the contents.

But they may miss the ideas that appear only once, like these:

Bonnet: Each [evaluation] question has a price tag, so I might split the budget in two and let each subcommittee [of the evaluation steering committee]—the "pros" and "cons"—decide how to invest their half in building their case. It would be up to them to work out the negotiations for questions that could turn out to support either side.

Eisner: [Educational connoisseurship and educational criticism] requires that classrooms be observed intensively in order to secure the kind of information that competent attention to classroom processes makes possible. Those processes when described, interpreted, and appraised in written narrative, have a family resemblance to the kind of writing that film, drama, and art critics create. The descriptive aspect . . . [enables] the readers to visualize what has transpired in classrooms . . . The interpretive aspect . . . attempts to account for what has transpired. . . . Finally, the evaluative aspect . . . renders some judgment on the educational value of what has been described and interpreted.

Popham: To get a firm fix on the board's likely satisfaction with my report, I would prepare in advance of data collection a *mock evaluation report* presenting admittedly fictitious data. Then I'd ask board members to see if there were omissions or redundancies in the content, structure, or style of the report.

Stake/Pearsol: Jim chose several students to observe closely. On each, he prepared a folder of anecdotes, hoping to show the humanities concepts and language they were acquiring. He checked with the people who knew these children to see how they were maturing intellectually. Attributing such gain to any particular lesson or course would be difficult, often impossible. Jim used the folders . . . in his interim report to the school board.

Webster: Ideally, the need for such a program would have been determined on the basis of input from the community, teachers, administrators, parents, and students, relative to services they wish their school system to provide. From the discrepancy between clients' desired services and those actually provided by the school district, a legitimate need for services is established.

Worthen: . . . I would envision collection of information on variables such as instances of in-school problems among different ethnic groups; membership in elective dance, drama, or art classes; museum attendance; and the like.

And from northern California, we get distinctive gropes of wrath.

Scriven: *Are you seriously suggesting that one can do an armchair evaluation of a multi-year, multi-instructor program?* Yes, occasionally. . . . Something like 75 percent of [students] will graduate higher in their college class than the average teacher. It is not appropriate to assume that a teacher of such modest academic competence can construct a curriculum linking and illuminating the most elusive and abstract and important concepts that the best minds of several millenia have evolved. It will be hard enough for most teachers to teach the notions from good texts, let alone in their spare time write the texts—which is what they have in essence done here.

Just to show that any list can be lengthened, here are a couple of distinctive gropes of my own.

• Spend Eisner's air fare on audiotapes of class discussions and ship them to him for analysis. (Don't send copies to Scriven; remember his aging heart.)

• Have a philosopher from Bryn Mawr College just down the road interview 20 students—10 from Radnor and 10 from Lower Merion (the district next door)—and say which are which.

8. Evaluators give report cards, too.

Report cards to parents should read one way; to teachers, another; to students, another; to administrators, another; to the general public, another; to the board, still another.

"Who is the report for?" is an excellent evaluation question. "Who are the reports for?" is an even better one. Statistics, background, conclusions, history, recommendations, diagnoses, instruments, analyses, alternatives, formulas, footnotes—they seldom belong in the same report.

And reports don't have to be in a single art form. They can be written, but need not be. They can be oral. They can be pictorial. They can be live demonstrations. They can be videotaped examples. And, in the case of Radnor, they can be danced, sung, or acted.

Reports can be short or long. But they should be as short as possible so someone will read, watch, or listen to them, especially if the board of education is the intended audience.

> **Eisner:** If the school board wanted this information for its confidential use—assuming I had permission from the teachers involved—I would write the report one way. If the report were to be read by the teachers *and* the board, it would be written differently. If it were to be used only by the teachers, it would be written still a third way. This chamelion-like approach to reporting rests on a simple premise: the aim of evaluation is to be helpful.

> **Popham:** I am a solid proponent of a less-is-more approach; evaluation reports should not be tomes, they should be teensies.

> **Bonnet:** There would be at least three written final reports. One would be a full technical report; although I'd make every effort to make it interesting, I wouldn't expect more than a handful of people to read it. Another would be ten or fifteen pages giving the findings in some detail and mentioning just enough about methods to give the study credibility. The third would be only a page or two.

9. There is no free evaluation.

ASCD wanted priceless evaluation designs. It got them by not setting a budget for the work.

An unbudgeted evaluation design problem is red meat (or pineapples) to evaluators. They react to it like teachers to a laundry list of goals without prices. Adrenalin flowing, eyes ablaze, stimulated by the competition, they grab Julia Child and head for the kitchen, where they cook up gourmet dishes. (ASCD hired only master chefs for this cookoff.)

But schools can't order from the left side of the menu. When Radnor takes a look at what the right sides of the menus in these chapters would have to be, it might have to go away hungry.

I refuse to talk to a school unless it will specify either: (1) the price it wants to pay, or (2) the work it wants done. If the school will name the price, I will specify the work. If the school will name the work, I will specify the price. Otherwise, if I am free to imagine both the price and the work, I go wild. I always come up with a design the school cannot afford. That wastes both their time and mine.

> **Popham:** A decent evaluative job would cost a fair amount of money, because we're talking about getting a fix on some rather elusive out-

comes. To get first-rate evaluators to spend a ton of time in the Radnor Township Schools—well, that's going to be difficult unless you pay them well. Now, if you want me to evaluate the humanities program in the Maui Middle School, I'd take on the assignment for a few pine-apples and, of course, travel expenses.

The Territory

As Tarzan said, with martini in hand resting in his tree house at the end of a very long day, "It's a jungle out there, Jane." Elephants live in the wild and so must those who appraise them.

10. Facts are rubber bullets.

Well, some facts persuade some people sometimes. But they are most persuasive when they prove what people already believe and least when they do the opposite. Some things are stronger than facts. Values are. A program grounded on the right values will not be washed away by a spate of facts showing that it doesn't work. High aspirations are. A program with its eyes set on the high hills, but whose feet are in fact immobile, will out-last one that aspires to move a mile and, in fact, moves a mile. Prior expectations are. If people associated with a program firmly expect it to do well or poorly or both, it will—for them.

Facts are rubber bullets. They can sting or stun an instructional pro-gram, but not kill it. Bad values, puny ambition, negative expectations—those can kill it. Still, everyone wants the facts. There is always the chance the truth will agree with what you believe.

> **Worthen:** . . . I always try to ferret out whether there is really any need to evaluate—that is, have those who hold the power to make the de-cision already made up their minds (with little probability they will change them), regardless of the results of the study? That perspective stems from the sad realization that perhaps 75 percent of my first several years as an evaluator was spent generating methodologically impeccable, but altogether useless evaluation reports—useless because I wasn't sharp enough to recognize the symptoms of ritualistic evalu-ation.

> **Webster:** Failure to meet objectives is often a necessary, but insufficient, reason to end a program.

11. Stakes aren't rare.

In public education, as in any public enterprise, decisions about the fate of a program are made by many—at least, influenced by many. There are stakeholders of every description and stakes of every description: students and learning, teachers and jobs, administrators and schedules, schools and prestige, school boards and money, parents and priorities. You can kill a program by driving a stake through its heart (sorry, Bob). Every experienced evaluator knows it, and every realistic evaluator accepts it.

> **Worthen:** I find formal decision makers seldom work in a vacuum and are often influenced by what standards other groups use to judge the program. I once tended to blurt out, within moments of an introductory handshake with a decision maker, "OK, now what criteria do you intend to use to determine whether or not to continue the program?" I am now more patient. Indeed, I like to share the full range of questions various groups hold to be important with the formal decision makers—in this case, the board—and ask them, in essence, whether the answer to that question would influence them to continue or scrap the program.

> **Stake/Pearsol:** Jim asked if the evaluation should be confined to board questions or could it consider questions raised by others. He was told to evaluate broadly—as long as the board's questions were answered. . . . One [central office] staff member put it this way, "I'd like to see us create a reading/writing lab instead, but with all this parent support for the humanities program, it would be political suicide to cut the program!"

> **Bonnet:** All of these groups are potential "audiences" of the evaluation because they all have a stake in the program—and possibly a voice in deciding its future . . . all of the school board members, the Radnor School principal, the Humanities Curriculum Review Committee, the humanities staff, other faculty leaders at Radnor School, central administrators with curricular influence, the principal and humanities faculty of the high school where Radnor students go, the principals of the elementary schools where Radnor students come from, Radnor School students, high school students who took the humanities course, Radnor School parent leaders, elementary and high school parent leaders, leaders in the community at large.

12. Evaluators aren't free agents.

People want evaluations to come out their way. And they are quite willing to press for their favorite conclusions.

> **Webster:** While this close relationship [between program personnel and the evaluator] is important, it is also essential that the evaluator retain independence from the program. Under no circumstances should the evaluator be assigned administratively to the program manager.

Scriven: *Why* take this tough a line? Because evaluation is not psychotherapy. When evaluators get on-site, we start holding hands, we get co-opted into other roles. But this is one case where the seduction of the savior role can be avoided.

I have never conducted an evaluation free of political pressure. Maybe it's my fault. Maybe I look like a bobbing cork? Or a raging bull in an oxcart parking lot? Either way, I inspire the client from the first interview, "Mitch, I'm concerned about how the thing will come out," to the last, "Mitch, I'll need to have a look at the report before it goes to the printer." On the other hand, maybe it isn't me. Maybe it's a cork and bull story familiar to many evaluators.

Appendix A.
A Short History of the Radnor Middle School Humanities Curriculum

by William P. Byrne and Mark A. Springer

William P. Byrne and Mark A. Springer are both teachers in the humanities department of Radnor Middle School, Wayne, Pennsylvania.

Foundations

The humanities curriculum at Radnor Middle School had its beginnings at the Symposium in Aesthetic Education held in Bucks County, Pennsylvania, in the summer of 1968. Two teachers, William Byrne and Charles Crawford, represented Radnor at the symposium.

Impressed with the related arts approach they learned that summer, Byrne and Crawford experimented with a new curriculum offered as a student activity during the 1968-69 school year. During the following summer, Radnor sent four more teachers to the symposium. Two of those teachers and Byrne and Crawford were given curriculum planning time in August 1969 to write "A Working Paper for a Course in Related Arts at the Middle School Level." During the 1969-70 school year, Byrne, Crawford, and another teacher piloted the program on a once-a-week basis in their seventh- and eighth-grade English classes.

In the summer of 1970, the Middle School Steering Committee approved the related arts course as a regular part of the middle school curriculum. The new program directly addressed four of the state's Ten Goals for Quality Education, aimed at helping every student: (1) search for answers to basic questions about life (Who am I? What is my role in society? What is my place in the physical universe?); (2) develop the skills of critical thinking; (3) understand and appreciate human achievements in the humanities, the social sciences and the natural sciences, and particularly those of his or her own heritage; and (4) develop understanding and appreciation of persons belonging to social, cultural, and ethnic groups different from his or her own.

The program was taught in all three grades for one trimester of the year. The remaining trimesters were devoted to theme-centered literature units. Crawford was appointed Coordinator of Humanities for the district and worked for a month developing teaching packets for English teachers who were as yet unfamiliar with the details of the related arts approach.

At the end of the 1970-71 school year, the program was again evaluated. A majority of the English teachers admitted that they were not comfortable with the related arts approach, and that they wanted to concentrate their efforts on teaching reading and writing skills. In light of this, the superintendent of schools commissioned Byrne, Crawford, and two other teachers to set up a separate humanities department.

During the summer of 1971, these teachers formulated a three-year curriculum based on the related arts approach with a heavy emphasis on literature. The single trimester of related arts separated from the thematic literature trimesters was scrapped in favor of the more integrated approach that continues to this day.

Early in its history, the humanities department, along with the other liberal arts areas, was involved in the writing, administration, and evaluation of a pre- and post-indicator under the direction of Research for Better Schools. Although this was primarily a teacher training experience, the humanities department used the results of this instrument in the further development of its curriculum.

In addition, the curriculum has undergone continual evaluation and revision. Each spring, for over a decade, all departments in the school have been required to submit goals and objectives for the next school year and a self-evaluation of how successfully they fulfilled their goals and objectives over the past year. This procedure has led to many improvements in the program.

The curriculum that was reviewed by the school board in October 1979, and which is the object of the evaluation strategies presented in this book, had thus evolved through ten years of teaching and countless hours of official and unofficial curriculum revision before the formal curriculum review proceedings were instigated.

Formal Program Evaluation

In the autumn of 1976, the Radnor Township School District introduced a Long-Range Plan of Curriculum Development Cycles in response to a state-wide mandate for curricular review. Under this five-year plan, each department in the district would undergo formal evaluation and, if necessary, revision in a three-phase cycle. These phases—planning, development, and implementation—would require a total of two or three years for each departmnt to complete. The department cycles were staggered throughout the five-year period from 1976-77 to 1981-82. In all cases a curriculum review committee was to be formed to conduct a needs assessment and to gather relevant information from research, visits, and interviews. The existing curriculum was then to be evaluated in light of the needs assessment and research findings. Phase two then allowed time for the committee to develop new units and materials to remedy any deficiences uncovered in the first phase. Finally, phase three consisted of the monitored implementation, or piloting, of these new curriculums. After a subsequent period of re-evaluation, the entire five-year sequence would begin again.

The humanities curriculum, however, differed from all others in at least two significant ways. First, it was not a districtwide, K-12 program, but existed only at the Radnor School. Second, while other programs were faced with revision, only the humanities program, by open admission of the school board, was faced with possible elimination.

Consequently, though the curriculum was not scheduled to begin its cycle until the fall of 1978, the humanities department staff decided in October 1976 to prepare for the cycle by rewriting its philosophy. Since all the central administrators and many of the school board members were relatively new to their posts, the department staff also decided to hold an informal meeting with the school board and the administration to familiarize them with the program.

Upon completion of these two measures in the spring of 1977, the administration suggested that the humanities staff find or develop a survey instrument that could quantitatively measure changes in the affective domain. Using information from the county information center, Research and Information Services for Education (RISE), it soon became apparent that no adequate instrument already existed, So, the department staff was allotted one week of summer work time to create one, along with a procedure for its implementation.

In September 1977, this homemade survey was administered to 100 Radnor Middle School students who had been selected by applying the table of random numbers to the alphabetical listings of students by grade. A neighboring school district of similar socioeconomic constitution agreed to let some of their students be used as a control group. However, to minimize disruption of their program, their sample was not randomly chosen. Instead, an "average" history class from each grade was given the survey. The results of this first survey were tabulated during the school year, and the survey was administered again to both sample groups in May 1978.

The overall results of the survey were mixed. In August 1978, the results and the indicator itself were reviewed in detail by the district's assistant superintendent, William Duffey, who judged them to be inconclusive. Problems experienced with the sample selection in the control group, poor testing situations in both groups, and a high attrition level in both samples by the May 1978 testing date affected the results to a statistically unacceptable degree. Duffey recommended that the results—both good and bad—be scrapped and that the entire process be redone, if tighter controls could be maintained.

Since these necessary controls could not be guaranteed, additional testing was postponed indefinitely. It was hoped at that point that the upcoming cycle would provide the time and the money to make possible a more acceptable testing situation.

In September 1978, the humanities curriculum went on cycle, and the district's assistant superintendent for instruction, James Holton, was appointed to head the cycle (curriculum review) committee. At the first meeting, held in October 1978, Holton announced to the department staff that the school board wanted the humanities cycle to be compressed from the normal two- or three-year allotment. All phases of the cycle were to be completed by April 1979, so the board could decide at that point if the program would be continued beyond the present school year. Eventually, this severely shortened timeline was expanded from seven months to 14 months, with a preliminary presentation to the school board scheduled for January 1979.

Between October 1978 and this first board presentation, the curriculum review committee was expanded to include three parents; 16 meetings were held; extensive research was done; and arrangements were made for visits to other school districts. All these efforts were directed at answering several questions the school board had deemed most pertinent: Why is this syncretic method of instruction appropriate for middle school students? How does this type of program reinforce reading and writing skills? How are programs of this sort implemented in other districts? Are the materials covered suitable for children of this age?

The presentation made to the board in January 1979 focused on these related issues. The board's reactions were mixed, and the committee was charged with several tasks: (1) Do more research on how students learn. (2) Examine more alternative structures. (3) Work on developing methods to increase emphasis on writing and literacy skills. (4) Expand the committee to include parents whose views differ from those of current members. (5) Increase input from the community and from other departments.

To fulfill these charges, the committee held 15 more meetings between February and May 1979. The committee was opened to all interested people and was then expanded to include four more parents, two of whom openly opposed the program, and five more teachers from other departments in the school. Additional meetings were held with other departments, with the middle school faculty as a whole, and with representatives from the elementary and high schools. An open public forum was also held.

At the same time, data collection was accelerated. Many school districts and ETS were contacted for information and another RISE search was initiated. Authorities at the University of Illinois were consulted on holonomic education, and visits were made to other schools to see how they implemented interdisciplinary courses. These sources provided additional material in support of the humanities program's philosophy.

The summer of 1979 was devoted to several interrelated endeavors. Though the staff's request for two weeks of paid summer work had been halved by the board, the four department members finished collating and reading the material gathered in the previous year, redesigned the structure and content of the curriculum in keeping with the information gained from these resources, and created a rough draft of the committee report.

In addition, three of the participants represented Pennsylvania in an NEH project concerning American Studies in Secondary Schools—an interdiciplinary project closely akin in its philosophy and structure to the Radnor humanities program. This project included the development of an American Studies unit to be placed within the framework of the humanities program.

That summer, two members of the humanities staff worked with teachers from the English and reading departments to develop a coordinated interdisciplinary unit on satire. This new unit was piloted during the 1979-80 school year as part of the new humanities curriculum.

During September and October 1979, the committee debated and polished its report to the school board, and planned the presentation format. The document was presented to the board at their October 23 meeting.

In many ways, the results of that meeting were inconclusive. Board members both for and against the program remained unchanged in their respective opinions about the humanities program, but they voted to postpone any final decision until a district philosophy of education could be developed and adopted by the board. Then, it was reasoned, the role of a program such as the humanities curriculum could be more effectively determined.

It is at this point that the authors of this book begin their "evaluations."

The program, in the form outlined in the October 1979 report (Appendix B) continues to exist as of this writing.

Appendix B.
Report of the Humanities Curriculum Review Committee

---

*After you understand all about the sun and the stars and
the rotation of the earth, you may still miss the radiance
of the sunset.*

—Alfred North Whitehead

Humanities: A Philosophical Overview

A major objective of any educational system should be to help each student
become more truly human; able to measure his or her own life against the ideals
valued by humankind. All students are entitled to an education that prepares
them for the fullest, richest possible life, by providing them with the opportunities and the skills required to achieve a clear understanding and appreciation
of all that it means to be human.

While this broad and liberal education certainly must include training in
reading, writing, and arithmetic, it must just as certainly go beyond these subjects. Clearly of equal importance are the fundamentally human questions of
meaning: the human concerns for personal and cultural traditions, and for
comprehending one's self, one's feelings, and one's relationships with others.
These are truly basic subjects of a meaningful and successful educational system. Today's facts may be tomorrow's trivia, but the ideals and values that
are the essence of humanity will remain.

Any educational system designed to realize this type of philosophy must
simultaneously reflect the philosophy in its methods as well as its content. The
system must be humanistic and student-centered. It must use practices that
strive to reach each student at that student's own levels of knowledge, abilities,
and feelings. It must employ techniques that embody the same dynamic
processes it intends to convey. Then, finally, it must do all of this while providing an atmosphere of genuine concern, support, and freedom.

From these fundamental beliefs, the members of the humanities department have compiled a list of general goals and one of specific objectives to fulfill this basic philosophy of education. Similarly, based on these goals and

objectives, we have developed a sequenced and syncretic* curriculum for all sixth, seventh, and eighth grade students. This curriculum is designed to provide each student with the widest possible range of experiences that enable students to recognize and comprehend values and meaning in many different media; and to communicate those values, along with their own, to others.

General Goals

Quality education should help every student search for answers to basic questions about life, such as: Who am I? What is my role in society? What is my place in the physical universe?

Quality education should help every student develop the skills of critical thinking.

Quality education should help every student understand and appreciate human achievement in the humanities, the social sciences and the natural sciences, particularly that of his or her own heritage.

Quality education should help every student understand and appreciate persons belonging to social, cultural, and ethnic groups different from his or her own.

Specific Objectives

The three-year humanities curriculum, designed as a unified and integrated whole, continually strives to:

• increase each student's aesthetic sensibility; that is, the ability to respond both affectively and cognitively to a variety of aesthetic experiences

• increase each student's proficiency in critical thinking skills, namely, the abilities to make and defend judgments; and in creative thinking, the abilities to select and synthesize to solve problems

• help each student understand and appreciate human achievements in the arts: literature, drama, film, music, the visual arts, architecture, and dance

• increase each student's understanding and appreciation of his or her own social, cultural, and ethnic group, while simultaneously helping him or her gain a greater understanding of, and appreciation for, the Judeo-Christian tradition, and the African and Oriental cultures

• help each student understand the interrelatedness that exists among seemingly disparate disciplines, and to help increase his or her ability to locate and describe patterns

• reinforce the student's oral and written communication skills.

I. Humanities Curriculum Objectives: A Summary

The goal of the humanities curriculum is to help each student acquire skills of disciplined inquiry, disciplined thinking, and disciplined expression in written and oral forms through a structured study of the related arts.

---

* Syncretic: characterized by the combination of different forms, using synthesis.

II. Humanities Curriculum Objectives: A Rationale

A. The humanities curriculum is intended for all students because all students are consumers of the arts, even if they never become producers of art.

B. The related arts are the core content focus because:

1. The arts are a significant and valuable portion of the human experience and should be an integral part of every student's basic education.

2. The arts are themselves interrelated, thus providing important opportunities for students to find and describe relationships among apparently different areas.

3. The arts provide a varied and interesting approach to the relationships that exist among all other disciplines; that is, they illustrate patterns of knowledge that need to be explored, in contrast to standard compartmentalization.

C. The skills of disciplined inquiry and thinking include those of looking for and recognizing patterns and forms—which is the essence of all learning—through such specific processes as analysis, synthesis, and evaluation.

D. The humanities curriculum constantly reinforces disciplined expression by requiring students to use written and oral communication skills correctly at all times.

III. The Committee's Recommendation Regarding Philosophy

A. After a discussion of the general philosophy and goals of the humanities curriculum, the 18-member committee voted unanimously that the program should continue to exist.

B. Similar sentiments were expressed by parents and other members of the general public at public meetings.

IV. The Committee's Recommendation Regarding Form

The committee believes that ideally a required, sequenced humanities program should span all levels K-12, but in the absence of that, the district should at least continue the program in its present form: two periods per week for all students in grades six, seven, and eight.

V. Rationale for the Committee's Recommendation on Form

A. Why the humanities should be required for all students:

1. All students are consumers of the arts and they need to develop their abilities to deal intelligently with the arts around them.

2. All students need and deserve both the reinforcement of basic skills and the opportunities to develop higher level thinking skills, which the humanities curriculum emphasizes.

3. Since the middle school is designed to be exploratory as well as preparatory, the overall school curriculum benefits from the diversity of experiences that this curriculum offers students.

4. The cohesive nature of the humanities program provides all middle school students with a shared set of common experiences.

5. This program could constitute some students' last formal exposure to the arts in general.

6. Similarly, the program may be the last one in which some students will be exposed to the interdisciplinary approach to learning and knowledge.

B. Why the humanities curriculum should have a three-year sequence:

1. The body of knowledge concerning the related arts is so immense that *at least* three years are needed.

2. A three-year sequence can better envelop and meet the multifaceted needs of students with individual learning styles.

3. Similarly, the three-year sequence more adequately accounts for learning differences due to age by allowing for the introduction and expansion of concepts suitable to the students' ages.

4. Since the middle school age is the age when the individual is moving away from the self-centered orientation of childhood into the increasing awareness of one's relationship to others and one's place in the larger world, humanities in a three-year sequence offers students a structured transition from involvement solely with self into knowledge and understanding of others.

C. Why humanities should be taught by a separate humanities department:

1. Other departments have the goals of their individual disciplines to achieve.

2. Other departments, such as the art department, recognize the importance of the goals of this program but lack the time to fulfill them and count on the present humanities department to do that.

3. There is a need in the education of every student for learning in individual disciplines and in interdisciplinary modes as well. An interdisciplinary department is not designed to replace other departments, but to reinforce and enhance the learning from all departments. Even if other departments were given the time and the humanities content divided among them, the essential value of the program would be lost because the interdisciplinary nature would necessarily disappear.

4. Information gathered by the committee shows that a nonrequired program not taught by a specifically designated staff falls by the wayside. This committee believes that the methods and materials are too valuable to lose by default.

VI. Committee Endorsement of the Recommendation on Form

The committee endorses continuation of the humanities curriculum to all students in grades six, seven, and eight by a separate department of teachers.

VII. Alternative Forms Explored

Before reaching the conclusion that the present form should continue, the committee looked into and discussed each of the following alternatives:

A. Three, four, or five periods per week, required in all three years.

B. Required for two periods per week in the sixth grade only, with elective humanities programs in the seventh and/or eighth grades.

C. Required for two periods per week in the sixth and seventh grades, with an elective program in the eighth grade.

D. Only as a seventh and/or eighth grade elective.

E. Only as a gifted seminar.

F. Various combinations of options A through E.

G. Taught by a single department five times per week for 12 weeks in each grade on a rotating trimester schedule with art, music, home economics, and industrial arts.

H. Taught by a team of teachers from other disciplines.

I. Humanities curriculum materials and objectives turned over to other disciplines to be taught on an optional/voluntary basis.

VIII. Rationales for Committee Rejection of Alternative Forms

All of the above alternatives were eliminated for one or more of the following reasons.

A. Alternatives that cut down on required time were eliminated because they cannot possibly fulfill the goals the committee deems essential.

B. Alternatives that involved scheduling as an elective were eliminated because of the committee's conviction that humanities is intended for all students.

C. Alternatives that entailed redistributing responsibilities to other disciplines were eliminated because:

   1. Such options are counter-productive to the interdisciplinary nature and purpose of the curriculum.

   2. The individual departments report that they have neither the time nor the facilities to implement the humanities curriculum adequately and fulfill their own goals at the same time.

   3. It has been observed in other schools that unless time and staff are specifically allocated, the success of interdisciplinary programs is jeopardized.

D. Alternative forms that would increase allocations of time for humanities were eliminated because of scheduling and staffing limitations.

E. Alternatives that involved a team of teachers from different disciplines were eliminated for the same reasons.

IX. The Committee's Recommendations Regarding Content

While the committee advocates continuing the present scheduling plan, we recognize the need for and value of changes in the content of the curriculum. In response to information we have collected from the school board, the public, students, teachers, administrators, outside specialists, and from our own observations, we propose the following content changes:

A. A new organizational framework for the program based on the concepts and skills being taught.

B. An increase in the number of formal writing assignments:
   1. Four formal writing assignments, written either in class or as homework, per pupil per trimester; each paper to be graded by the teacher, corrected by the student, signed by the parent, and kept on file with the teacher.
   2. The additional requirement of a written section in every project.
   3. An increase in the number of written projects required.

C. An increase in the number and frequency of informal writing assignments.

D. Heightened emphasis on the quality of formal oral presentations by the students.

E. Increased emphasis on literature and literary concepts.

F. Increased emphasis on vocabulary development.

G. Increased number of objective tests, particularly in grades seven and eight.

H. Introduction of an A, B, C, D, U grading system to replace the E, S, U system currently in use.

I. Increased coordination with other departments.

X. New Conceptual Framework for the Content

The following outline of concepts has been developed to clarify the specific objectives of the humanities curriculum. New lesson plans to implement these concepts are presently being written. They illustrate as well the ways in which the other recommended improvements will be facilitated. These lesson plans are available for examination.

Sixth-Grade Humanities: The Artist Looks at the Humanities

Unit One: How do we communicate with each other?

 I. What is necessary for communication?
   A. Two or more people
   B. A purpose: Why do we need to communicate?
   C. A message or meaning
   D. A form or medium

 II. How do we communicate?
   A. Nonverbally
      1. Movement/dance: How do we communicate with movement?
      2. Signs/art: How do we communicate with signs and symbols?
      3. Sound/music: How do we communicate with music?
   B. Verbally
      1. How do we communicate with words?
      2. How do we communicate with literature?

Unit Two: What is a work of art?

I. *What is a definition of a work of art? (the skillful manipulation of elements and principles into relationships to create a meaningful whole that has impact and significance)*
  A. *Why must art be created and organized by humans?*
  B. *How can art be more than useful? (impact and significance)*
  C. *How is skill involved in art?*

II. *What are the forms that art can take?*
  A. *Literature*
  B. *Drama*
  C. *Painting and photography*
  D. *Sculpture*
  E. *Architecture*
  F. *Music*
  G. *Dance*
  H. *Film and television*

III. *What major elements and principles are present in each of the art forms?*
  A. *Which art forms use color?*
  B. *Which forms use line?*
  C. *Which art forms use shape?*
  D. *Which forms use texture?*
  E. *Which forms use space?*
  F. *Which use balance?*
  G. *Which use rhythm?*

IV. *How are all the elements and principles arranged into a total composition?*

V. *How can we create an A-B-A composition?*

Unit Three: How does a work of art express its artist's individual style?

I. *What is style? What is an artist's individual style?*
  A. *The way something is done that makes it unique.*
  B. *The way the artist manipulates the elements and principles to make his or her work unique.*

II. *What is style in poetry?*
  A. *Subject matter*
  B. *Figurative language*
  C. *Rhyme*
  D. *Rhythm*
  E. *Typography*
  F. *Diction*
  G. *And other elements*

III. What is style in music?

IV. What is style in painting?

V. How do we recognize an individual artist's style?

VI. How do I describe an individual artist's style?

Unit Four: How does a work of art portray character?

   I. What is character? (a real or imagined personality)

   II. How do we discover character?
     A. Physical appearance
     B. The way the individual acts
     C. What the individual says
     D. What others say about the individual

III. How are personae delineated in the arts?
     A. How do short-story writers delineate character?
     B. How do dramatists portray character?
     C. How do poets portray character?
     D. How do composers portray characters in music?
     E. How do film-makers portray character?
     F. How do painters portray character?

IV. How do I create and express a character?

V. How does a work of art portray characters in relation to one another?

Seventh-Grade Humanities: The Artist Looks at Society

Unit One: American cultural perceptions of aging (an American Studies pilot unit developed for the National Endowment for the Humanities)

   I. What is American Studies?

   II. Who are the elderly?

III. When is a person old?

IV. How were the elderly perceived in colonial America, 1607-1780?
     A. What were the historical perspectives of the time?
     B. What evidence can we get from the poetry and literature of the era?
     C. What evidence can we get from primary sources, such as sermons, from that era?

V. How were the elderly perceived during the time of American expansion, 1780-1870?
     A. What were the historical perspectives of that era?
     B. What evidence can we get from the literature of that era?

C. *What evidence can we get from the paintings of that era?*

D. *What have professional sociologists and cultural anthropologists said about American perceptions of aging in this time period?*

VI. *How were the elderly perceived during the period from 1870 through 1920?*

  A. *What are the historical perspectives from the time period?*

  B. *What evidence can we get from the arts of that era?*

  C. *What evidence can we get, or conclusions can we draw, from statistical demographic and economic data from that era?*

VII. *How have the elderly been perceived in the modern period, 1920 to the present?*

  A. *What are the historical perspectives of the time period?*

  B. *What evidence can we get from the arts of the time period?*

  C. *What is "stereotyping?"*

  D. *What are the predominant stereotypes regarding the elderly in modern America?*

  E. *What conclusions concerning the validity of these stereotypes can we draw from statistical data and primary source materials?*

Unit Two: How do works of the art reflect their times?

I. *What is style in the arts (a review)*

II. *What is period style?*

III. *What are the traditional art periods?*

  A. *When and where did they take place?*

  B. *What historical events were occurring at the time?*

IV. *How are works of art in a given time period similar?*

  A. *How are paintings similar in a given time period?*

  B. *How are works of sculpture similar in a given time period?*

  C. *How is the architecture of a time period similar?*

  D. *How is the music of a time period similar?*

  E. *How can we describe the relationships among these art forms in a given time period?*

V. *How are the art works of two time periods different?*

  A. *How are the paintings of two time periods different?*

  B. *Sculpture?*

  C. *Architecture?*

  D. *Music?*

  E. *What can these differences tell us about the general differences between the two time periods?*

Unit Three: How do works of art reflect the ways cultures view the world?

    I. What are the universal components of all cultures?

        A. Cultural background

        B. Themes

        C. Economics

        D. Food, clothing, shelter

        E. Family

        F. Political organization

        G. Attitude toward the unknown

        H. Communication

        I. Arts and aesthetic values

        J. Recreation

    II. How do the Western, Japanese, and West African cultures view the world?

        A. What are the tenets of pantheistic religions?

        B. What are the tenets of Buddhism?

        C. What are the tenets of monotheistic religions?

    III. How are these world views similar and different?

    IV. How do the arts of these cultures communicate their respective world views?

Unit Four: How do works of art use satire to comment on human nature?

    I. What is satire?

    II. What are the components of satire?

        A. Satiric norm

        B. Satiric target

        C. Satiric vehicle

    III. What form does satire take?

        A. What is sarcasm?

        B. What is irony?

        C. What is parody?

    IV. How have satirists looked at specific topics?

        A. How have satirists looked at manners and mores?

        B. How have satirists looked at education?

        C. How have satirists looked at technology?

Eighth-Grade Humanities: The Artist Looks at the Universe

Unit One: How are scientific thought and changes in technology influenced by the arts?

  I. *What is the relation between art and science?*
    A. *How did da Vinci illustrate the relationship between art and science?*

 II. *What are some of the major theories of mankind and the universe that have altered the arts?*
    A. *What is geocentricity?*
    B. *What is heliocentricity?*
    C. *What are the basic theories of Newton?*
    D. *What are the basic theories of Einstein?*

III. *How did Newton's theories influence the arts of the 18th and 19th centuries?*
    A. *What were the historical events occurring in that time?*
    B. *What were the major trends of patterns in social thought at the time?*
    C. *What was the state of the arts at the time?*
    D. *How are these three aspects interrelated?*

IV. *How have Einstein's theories influenced the arts of the 20th century?*
    A. *What were the major historical events of the time?*
    B. *What were the major trends of patterns in social thought at the time?*
    C. *What was the state of the arts?*
    D. *How are all these aspects interrelated?*

 V. *What are some of the major inventions that have revolutionized the arts?*
    A. *How did the printing press influence the arts?*
    B. *How did the camera influence the arts?*
    C. *How did steel influence the arts?*
    D. *How has the laser influenced the arts?*

VI. *What possible effects might future technology have on the arts?*

Unit Two: What kind of worlds have artists created?

  I. *What purposes can created worlds serve?*
    A. *To entertain*
    B. *To teach*
      1. *To comment on the real world*
      2. *To improve the real world*
    C. *To warn*

 II. *Into what categories can we divide these worlds?*
    A. *Science fiction*
    B. *Fantasy*

C. *Utopias*

III. *How does a novelist create a fantasy world?*

IV. *How can we use the universal components of a culture to create a world?*

Unit Three: What is the creative process?

I. *What are the types of thinking processes?*
   A. *What is a dichotomy?*
   B. *What is convergent thinking?*
   C. *What is divergent thinking?*
   D. *What are inductive and deductive reasoning?*
   E. *What are fluency and flexibility?*

II. *How do these types of thinking processes influence the creative process?*

Unit Four: How do we evaluate a work of art?

I. *What is a critical review?*
   A. *A disciplined expression of an evaluation of an art work, based on careful inquiry and thought, backed by supporting details.*

II. *What criteria are used to judge a work of art?*
   A. *Skill: artistry and order using the elements and principles*
   B. *Impact: lasting importance to the individual*
   C. *Significance: lasting importance to the culture*

III. *Who determines a classic?*
   A. *Who decides?*
      1. *Critical consensus*
      2. *Lasting audience*
      3. *Proven significance*
   B. *What is the difference between objective aesthetic judgment and personal taste?*

IV. *How do I use the established criteria to evaluate a work of art?*

V. *How do I clearly express my evaluation as a review?*

VI. *How do I read and respond to reviews by others?*

ASCD Publications, Fall 1981

Yearbooks

A New Look at Progressive Education
(610-17812) $8.00
Considered Action for Curriculum Improvement
(610-80186) $9.75
Education for an Open Society
(610-74012) $8.00
Evaluation as Feedback and Guide
(610-17700) $6.50
Feeling, Valuing, and the Art of Growing:
Insights into the Affective
(610-77104) $9.75
Life Skills in School and Society
(610-17786) $5.50
Lifelong Learning—A Human Agenda
(610-79160) $9.75
Perceiving, Behaving, Becoming: A New Focus
for Education (610-17278) $5.00
Perspectives on Curriculum Development
1776-1976 (610-76078) $9.50
Schools in Search of Meaning
(610-75044) $8.50
Staff Development/Organization Development
(610-81232) $9.75

Books and Booklets

About Learning Materials (611-78134) $4.50
Action Learning: Student Community Service
Projects (611-74018) $2.50
Adventuring, Mastering, Associating: New
Strategies for Teaching Children
(611-76080) $5.00
Applied Strategies for Curriculum Evaluation
(611-81240) $5.75
Approaches to Individualized Education
(611-80204) $4.75
Bilingual Education for Latinos
(611-78142) $6.75
Classroom-Relevant Research in the Language
Arts (611-78140) $7.50
Clinical Supervision—A State of the Art Review
(611-80194) $3.75
Curriculum Leaders: Improving Their Influence
(611-76084) $4.00
Curriculum Materials 1981 (611-81266) $5.00
Curriculum Theory (611-77112) $7.00
Degrading the Grading Myths: A Primer of
Alternatives to Grades and Marks
(611-76082) $6.00
Developmental Supervision: Alternative
Practices for Helping Teachers Improve
Instruction (611-81234) $5.00
Educating English-Speaking Hispanics
(611-80202) $6.50
Effective Instruction (611-80212) $6.50
Elementary School Mathematics: A Guide to
Current Research (611-75056) $5.00
Eliminating Ethnic Bias in Instructional
Materials: Comment and Bibliography
(611-74020) $3.25
Global Studies: Problems and Promises for
Elementary Teachers (611-76086) $4.50
Handbook of Basic Citizenship Competencies
(611-80196) $4.75
Humanistic Education: Objectives and
Assessment (611-78136) $4.75
Learning More About Learning
(611-17310) $2.00
Mathematics Education Research
(611-81238) $6.75

Measuring and Attaining the Goals of Education
(611-80210) $6.50
Middle School in the Making
(611-74024) $5.00
The Middle School We Need
(611-75060) $2.50
Moving Toward Self-Directed Learning
(611-79166) $4.75
Multicultural Education: Commitments, Issues,
and Applications (611-77108) $7.00
Needs Assessment: A Focus for Curriculum
Development (611-75048) $4.00
Observational Methods in the Classroom
(611-17948) $3.50
Open Education: Critique and Assessment
(611-75054) $4.75
Partners: Parents and Schools
(611-79168) $4.75
Professional Supervision for Professional
Teachers (611-75046) $4.50
Reschooling Society: A Conceptual Model
(611-17950) $2.00
The School of the Future—NOW
(611-17920) $3.75
Schools Become Accountable: A PACT
Approach (611-74016) $3.50
The School's Role as Moral Authority
(611-77110) $4.50
Selecting Learning Experiences: Linking
Theory and Practice (611-78138) $4.75
Social Studies for the Evolving Individual
(611-17952) $3.00
Staff Development: Staff Liberation
(611-77106) $6.50
Supervision: Emerging Profession
(611-17796) $5.00
Supervision in a New Key (611-17926) $2.50
Urban Education: The City as a Living
Curriculum (611-80206) $6.50
What Are the Sources of the Curriculum?
(611-17522) $1.50
Vitalizing the High School (611-74026) $3.50
Developmental Characteristics of Children and
Youth (wall chart) (611-75058) $2.00

**Discounts on quantity orders of same title to
single address: 10-49 copies, 10%; 50 or more
copies, 15%. Make checks or money orders
payable to ASCD. Orders totaling $20.00 or
less must be prepaid. Orders from institutions
and businesses must be on official purchase
order form. Shipping and handling charges will
be added to billed purchase orders. *Please be
sure to list the stock number of each publication, shown in parentheses.*

Subscription to *Educational Leadership*—$18.00
a year. ASCD Membership dues: Regular (subscription [$18] and yearbook)—$34.00 a year;
Comprehensive (includes subscription [$18]
and yearbook plus other books and booklets
distributed during period of membership)—
$44.00 a year.**

Order from:

**Association for Supervision and
Curriculum Development
225 North Washington Street
Alexandria, Virginia 22314**

3449

375.006
Ap 58

121293